DEDICATION

This book is dedicated to the professional salesperson who devotes their time and energy to the task of helping patients, clients, or customers with their product or service. Chances are better than not that I'm speaking of you.

. . . With love, I also dedicate this book to my best friend after over 62 years of marriage!

To Jean

Have I told you you're the most important person in my life?

Have I told you I'm so lucky to have you for my wife?

Have I told you all the many, many things you are to me?

Well, just in case I haven't lately; let me mention two or three.

You're the sunshine in my morning; you're the smile upon my face.

You're the lover in my evening, in your gowns of silk and lace.

You're the sweet scent of the flower that I stop to smell.

It is your strength that gives me power that I shall never fail.

Did I tell you when I found you; you were the object of my cares?

Did I tell you when I found you; you were the answer to my prayers?

Did I tell you that I loved you, oh so long ago?

Well, just in case I haven't told you lately, it's time I let you know.

I love you because your kind to every living thing.

I love your positive mind and all the happiness you bring.

I love you, you're my best friend, and that you'll always be.

And, most of all I love you for the way that you love me.

- Roy

A TRIBUTE TO MY HERO!

As a kid, one of my first memorable experiences was going to the movies to watch King of the cowboys, Roy Rogers. Gene Autry was the first singing cowboy in the movies. Roy Rogers was the second. Roy was number one in the box office for twelve years. Roy rode a beautiful golden palomino Roy named Trigger. Dale Evans starred with Roy and the gruffy, Gabby Hayes. My name being Roy, I always played the part of Roy Rogers, when we, as kids, played Cowboys and Indians. Roy Rogers became my childhood hero, and I spent my days playing "the good guy!" What a great training program for a child. After TV came on the scene, Roy, Dale, Trigger, and a dog named Bullet had a daily program on which they taught all the young kids the importance of being honest and always treating others with kindness. They opened and closed their show singing a song written by Dale called,

"Happy Trails to You!"

As an adult, I became a hearing aid salesperson and soon began to manufacture hearing aids. Television celebrity Art Linkletter was our company spokesman. Roy Rogers had a loss of hearing and after Art introduced me to Mr. Rogers, I fitted him with hearing aids. I soon discovered that he was the wonderful hero I had envisioned him to be. Over the next 20 years, Roy and I went to lunch twice a month and became best of friends.

After four years our wives, Dale and Jean joined Roy and me at lunch. Roy leaned towards me and asked, *"How would you like me to* endorse your hearing aids?" Of course, I said yes and asked him if I should contact his agent, Art Rush. Roy replied,

"No! I thought I could say, ever since I got my Nu-Ear hearing aids, I hear every word the minister speaks, every note the choir sings, and Dale doesn't have to holler at me anymore!"

I said, "WOW, that's great Roy," and I asked him, "How would you like me to pay you?" Roy put his arm on my shoulder and said, "You are my friend, don't worry about it!"

Roy was driving as we headed back to the museum. He stopped at a corner, turned to me, and said, "If you had ever asked me to endorse your hearing instruments, I had a plan as to how I was going to tell you <u>no</u>. It's because you never asked that I decided to do it." Roy gave me complete use of his good name and unparalleled reputation and never charged me a dime. I have always considered that Roy Rogers placing that much trust in me was the greatest honor I have ever received. He was the greatest of friends!

Happy trails to you, Roy Rogers!

Playing cowboys with Roy!

CONTENTS

INTRODUCTION

Look around you. Everything you see has been sold to someone by someone. The product or service regardless of its size, shape or even its value was purchased to fill some persons need or maybe more important some persons want. The products and services were sold at a profit creating income to many. The many, with paycheck in hand were off to the marketplace to fulfill their needs and wants by being sold products and services by others, and the cycle goes on.

Our economy is built on this process, and little happens until someone sells something to someone. The selling process is simply, *"Find a person with a need or want and provide a service or product to satisfy it."* While satisfying the patient, the client or the customer's needs and wants may seem simple, it's not always easy.

I shall hereafter refer to the patient, the client, and the customer as the *"prospective buyer."* And I shall refer to the seller as the *"salesperson."* The prospective buyer has much to consider. "Which is the best product or service, from whom should I purchase it, and what is a fair price?" Will it fulfill my need, and can I afford to purchase it?" These are just a few of the many questions that must be answered before a purchase happens. Questions are often presented as "OBJECTIONS" to be overcome, and only after you have answered the questions, you may then,

... *"Close the Sale!"*

Please note that in this book I prefer to use the time-honored marketing term *"closing the sale."* I am aware that *"closing the sale"* can be considered a hard term, however it is also hard to misunderstand its meaning. Regardless of terminology, the salesperson is obligated to perform in a manner consistent with a professional standard. If one's purpose is to offer a product or service to an individual needing that product or service, then nothing is gained if the prospective buyer does not purchase the product or service he or she needs. The sale must be closed in one way or another, so that each party benefits. The words *"closing the sale"* should not imply that the individual was sold a product or service that was inappropriate or unneeded. Such unprofessional behavior is an ethical issue unrelated to the concept of closing a sale for a useful product or service. There is never a reason to deceive or lie to the prospective buyer! Motivating a prospective buyer to purchase a needed product or service is not deception! Especially when putting-off the purchase may cause the need to worsen.

"The difference between motivation

and manipulation…is intent!"

And maybe the greatest motivator of all is PAIN! No one desires surgery but, sometimes it's the best option to relieve the pain. When need is accompanied by pain as a motivation, closing the sale is not an issue. Most other needs or wants require gentle persuasion.

Throughout my career, I have been researching the closing techniques of many professional top persuaders. In this book, I encapsulate those secrets that have set these people apart and made them the best at what they do. I have learned that each of us is motivated by different desires. Some will profess that their <u>only</u> reason for being in their profession is to help those who need their product or service. They claim money has no influence on their actions; they are motivated only by helping others. Hard to argue with such an honorable motive. If your only goal is to help others, don't fail,

. . . *Close the Sale!*

There are others who are motivated by their financial gains. They see their profession as a great way to make a living. Making a living is necessary and being financially successful is not a fault. Making money and being a good provider for your family is a virtue of which one should be proud. There's nothing wrong with becoming financially successful thus allowing you to send your children to college, take vacations, and build a fund for retirement. If financial success is your purpose, don't fail,

. . . *Close the Sale!*

It is my belief that there are many preplanned motives necessary to maintain a successful lifestyle. I described the plan as a "triangle of success." All triangles have three points and each of the three points of this triangle represents an important goal to develop a successful career.

- **Plan to help others,**

- **Plan to make money, and**

- **Plan to have fun while doing it!**

The triangle is slowly spinning. At any given time, one point of the triangle may be more important than the other two, but each is essential to our success. If your desire is to help others, and you do so, the good news is, *"You will probably make money."* The more people you help, the more money you will make. On the other hand, if your desire is to make money, *"you will undoubtedly help people."* And . . . helping people and making money are both fun. One thing for sure, irrespective of your motive, nothing will be accomplished if you don't,

    . . . Close the Sale!

Welcome to **"The Gentle Art of Persuasion!"**

    Gathering sales expertise by learning from another salespersons successful experiences will help you to motivate others to purchase that which they need or want and at the same time dramatically increase your income. If you read this entire book and receive only *one* idea, *one* technique, *one* story that works for you, your time will have been well spent. *One* sales idea that will help you to overcome an objection and close a sale used hundreds or thousands of times throughout your career will not only help satisfy the needs and wants of those in your trust but, could also help satisfy your financial needs and wants. You can have that which you need or want by helping others acquire that which they need or want,

    . . . Does that make sense to you?

ABOUT THE AUTHOR

Who wrote this book and do his ideas really work? Has he walked the walk before he has talked the talk? Those are good questions which need answering before you spend your valuable time reading. It makes no sense to follow the suggestions of an instructor who can't do it. And besides, these questions give me a chance to brag a little. At the age of nine I lived in Gonzales, California, a small farming community a hundred or so miles south of San Francisco. During the summer, at roughly four a.m. each morning a two and a half-ton converted army truck stopped a block from our rented family home. My mother, two brothers, two sisters and I along with a group of migrant farm workers boarded the truck and left for work.   I'll always remember the milk can that was welded in the back of the truck from which we all drank using the same long dipper all day. We spent the day topping garlic, bundling carrots, or thinning sugar beets. The work was hard, the pay was poor. I learned this phrase from some of the Mexican workers. *"Mucho trabajo y poco dinero"* meaning *"Much work and little money!"* Topping garlic paid nineteen cents a box and my mother would allow me to go home as soon as I filled ten boxes, which took me until noon. Going home meant walking through the fields to the nearest highway and then thumbing a ride to town. There were always ripe vegetables left in the fields after picking so by the time my brother, Don who was six and I reached the highway we were often toting a crate of broccoli, lettuce, or onions. Considering we were dirty, smelled of garlic, and had a messy load it's no wonder most of our rides were in the back of a pick-up truck. Once we arrived home, we would pack our goods in our little red wagon and sell them to our neighbors. It was at that early age; I learned the importance of selling and I learned that I could make a lot more money selling than I could working in the fields. When I was eleven, the family moved to Salt Lake City, and I got a job selling newspaper subscriptions, door-to-door, for the Salt Lake Tribune/Telegram. At sixteen, I accepted a position selling 3-Ply stainless steel cookware. I learned the demo primarily so I could present it in my high school sales class. The teacher was so impressed she purchased a complete set of cookware from me. During the following summer her husband, a college graduate, started selling cookware under my tutelage. What I learned that summer was that I didn't have to have a college education to hire someone who did. At the time I believed that *"some people had to quit school at the high school level so they could start a business and have jobs ready for those who went on to college."* When you want a good lifestyle and your academic skills are not great, your options are limited. The best option for me was to go into business for myself. When I told them about my plans, my parents said I was a dreamer, which inspired me to write this poem:

Dream

Do a little dreaming, each and every day.

Reach for a distant star, though it seems so far away.

Your dreams become your goals, brought to action by a plan.

And your plan becomes achievable the day you say, "I can."

So do a little dreaming, of what your future is to be.

A successful life you'll find is a self-fulfilling prophecy.

As a wish becomes reality, it is time to wish anew.

So do a little dreaming, and you'll have a dream come true.

When I was twenty, I returned home from the Army. A friend and I opened a small café we named "The Snack Shack." The café business required us to work hard for long hours and produced little profit. Once again, *"Mucho trabajo y poco dinero."* One day, the person for whom I had sold newspaper subscriptions, invited me to accompany him as he sold hearing aids. On that Saturday in 1960, at the age of twenty-one, I found myself selling hearing aids to the hearing impaired. At twenty-three I ran the sales portion of the national training center for Beltone, the world's largest hearing aid and hearing test equipment company. At the time I developed the sales presentation that became the standard for most of the nation's hearing aid dispensers.

Selling hearing aids, door-to-door, was not an easy sale back then. A hearing aid was body worn with a cord that had an ear molded button on the end that fit into the ear. Men wore the hearing aid attached to the underside of their tie and women wore theirs in their bra. If a person had a serious impairment, they were a relatively "easy sale." Unfortunately, those early hearing aids were not strong enough to fit a serious loss of hearing. And those who had a mild to moderate loss of hearing would not admit they had a loss; they blamed others. They claimed people didn't speak loud enough and they mumbled.

"We were selling a product that no one wanted to people who would not admit they needed one!"

If a person walked with the help of a red and white cane, everyone came to their aid. Their impairment was apparent, and others were compassionate and wanted to help them. There were no outward signs that accompanied a loss of hearing, the hearing impaired looked normal while the loss had a devastating effect on their life. Helen Keller lost her <u>sight</u> and <u>hearing</u> after a bout of scarlet fever at the age of nineteen months. She became the first deaf and blind person to earn a Bachelor of Arts degree. She often commented that the loss of hearing was worse than the loss of sight. She once said,

"When you lose your sight,

you lose contact with things.

When you lose your hearing,

you lose contact with people!"

Playing the TV so loud that everyone with normal hearing leaves the room and being asked to repeat oneself over and over by hearing, "What did you say?" as an answer to every question was annoying to family and friends. As time passed electronics miniaturized and hearing aids were built into the temples of eyeglasses. First Lady, Eleanor Roosevelt had a loss of hearing and in 1955 was fitted with a set of the very first *eyeglass* hearing aids. They were large and cumbersome to wear and added at least ten years to Eleanor's appearance. A hearing aid became a sign of old age. Later came the behind-the-ear and eventually all-in-the-ear hearing aids. As the product improved the selling process also improved.

Fourteen years later, at the age of thirty-five, I was a millionaire, operating a retail hearing-aid business. Fifteen years later I founded Nu-Ear Electronics and developed an "Open House" program that was credited for helping millions of hearing-impaired people with better hearing. I have been introduced at seminars held throughout the United States as, *"The World's Best Hearing Aid Salesperson!"* Believe me I am very proud of that accolade. I am also proud that I was often introduced as, *"The Hearing Aid fitter of The Stars!"* A few of the stars whom I helped either they or a member of their family with their hearing included my friend Roy Rogers, Art Linkletter, Jack Benny, Chuck Norris, Gary Busey, Grandpa Jones, Tommy and Virl Osmond, Roy Clark, Waylon Jennings, Buddy Hackett, Dub Taylor, Patrick Macnee, Charlton Heston, Art Carney, and many others. I achieved financial success by selling better hearing to people who needed the benefits of what I sold. I got what I wanted by helping others get what they wanted only because I learned how to overcome objections and,

. . . Close the Sale!

I am truly excited to share with you a few time-tested secrets, certainly not all my own, and if applied properly they will work for anyone. I may present answers to objections to a few questions related only to the hearing aid profession hoping they may be transposed for your purpose.

Thank you for taking time to read my book. I feel a great sense of obligation to give you something in return. It is therefore my sincere hope that you come away with many new and different persuasion ideas, but I will be pleased if you find just _one_ good idea that is easy to use and works well for you. New ideas may not really be new at all. Some have been around for years, but when they first came to your attention, you may not have been ready to hear them. I hope you will come away thinking that most of my thoughts are basic, self-evident, and easy to understand and apply. As you read, remember that the mind, like a parachute, works a whole lot better when it is fully opened.

You may still question if the ideas represented here really work. Before you read on, consider the following story:

> There once was a man who, each morning, stopped by
> the local jewelry store and meticulously set his watch to
> the big clock in the window. One such morning, the
> jeweler commented, "Boy, time sure must be important to
> you. I see you here setting your watch every morning." The

man replied, *"Yes, it is. I work at the factory, and I must blow the whistle to let everyone off for lunch. It must blow on time."*

"Funny thing," the jeweler said, *"all these years, I have been setting that clock in the window to the time that whistle blows."*

Obviously, there is a probability of error. When you follow another person's lead, be sure he or she is going where you wish to be. Don't become a follower, following a follower!

Often a salesperson will say they have 10 to 12 years' experience at that which he or she does, when what they really have had is only one year of learning experience and they have done it for 10 to 12 years.

If you are a doctor, a lawyer, an engineer, a businessperson, a waitress, a hair stylist, and especially if you are a professional salesperson, The "Gentle Art of Persuasion" has been written for you! No matter how educated and skillful you are at your profession, you will be more successful if you acquire a greater ability to communicate, and...

"You don't have to be sick to get better."

CHAPTER ONE

Change is the Price We Must Pay for Progress!

"Continue to think how you've always thought,

and you'll continue to get what you've

always got!"

You don't go from start to smart in your profession without making a few mistakes, and all too often your mistakes become your habits. Your habits become your character, and your character dictates your destiny!

Change does not come easy! The only person, seemingly, who really likes to change, is a baby with a dirty diaper. For most of the rest of us, change can be scary. We stay with what we know, the way things are, which is the status-quo. Change usually means jumping out of our rut, running along the edge for a short period of time, and then falling back into our rut to maintain the status quo. If you were a non-achiever in high school and you haven't changed your approach, you're probably a non-achiever in life.

Your good friend proclaims: "I'm going to stop smoking!" or "I'm going to stop drinking!" Or how about, "I'm going to lose some weight!" You see your friend a week later, and he or she says, "I'm on my seventh day without a ___!" When you see your friend the next week, he or she is eating french fries, smoking a cigarette, and having a drink to celebrate the fact he or she's back in the rut, where he or she is again comfortable. He or she had good intentions, but poor results.

Sir Isaac Newton said,

"A body in motion will stay in motion,"

to which I add,

"Even if a body is going in the wrong direction."

We all love it when we get something right, and in a world where people argue about every little thing, where everyone thinks differently, and change is the only certainty, getting it right reaffirms our intellect, like when we work our way through a puzzling problem to a resoundingly correct solution. Not everyone can do this, you know!

While most of us would like to change the way we do a few things, it has been my observation that few people have been taught how to change.

The process of changing has 5 necessary steps:

Step 1: You must have, *"A strong desire to change."*

H.L. Hunt, owner of more than two hundred companies and at one time the richest man in the world, was once asked on a radio interview for his "secret to success." He replied, "I have found that there are only three things necessary for success."

"First, decide exactly what you want.

Second, determine the price you must pay to get it.

and Third, resolve to pay that price."

What is your sales closing rate? 20%? 30%? 50%? Maybe it's 90%? How important is it for you to improve? If you are at 30% and you improve to 60%, how would that change your lifestyle? If you doubled your closing rate, would it not double the number of people you are helping? And would it not double your income? Can you become passionately involved in changing for the better? Do you have a strong desire to make it happen? If not, toss this book, it will only waste your time and irritate you because it will no doubt challenge the way you think, and of course, at this point, you believe the way you think is right!

"The child is the parent of the adult!"

Now, what do I mean by that? Considering that the human computer is self-programming; a great deal of what you believe to be true today was put there by you, many years ago, at a time when you were not as smart as you are today. So, you as a child established many of the truths that you now, as an adult, believe and use as a guide for making many of the important decisions by which you live.

Does the phrase...

"Because I've always done it that way!"

... Ring a bell?

I once heard the great motivational speaker, **Zig Ziglar** tell a story about a newly married couple who were about to cook a ham. As he prepared to place the ham into the oven, his wife said, *"Wait, you forgot to cut the end off the ham."* When he asked why he should cut the end off the ham she stated, *"Any good cook knows you must cut the end off the ham."* Her explanation bothered her husband and he again asked, *"why?"* She said, *"I'm not sure but, mom is a good cook, and she always cuts the end off the ham."* They called mom, who said, *"Any good cook knows you must cut the end off the ham."* But *"Why?"* her son-in-law asked. She answered, *"I'm not sure but, my mom is a great cook, and she always cuts the end off the ham."* So, they called Grandma, who explained, *"The reason I cut the end off the ham is that I have a small pan!"*

How much of your thinking today is influenced by the fact that your mentor had a small pan?

Isn't this a great time to rethink possibilities, and recapture dreams? Isn't this a great time for "updating" a little of your computer programming? Wouldn't it make good sense for you, the parent, to get back into control? Think of the possibilities. You could program yourself to change habits which no longer serve your purpose. You might even program yourself to stop smoking, quit drinking, or maybe to lose a few pounds. And yes,

You can program yourself to do better when you,

   ... *Close The Sale!*

How are we doing? How's your "want" intensity? Do you really want to be better at,

   ... *Closing the Sale?*

If your **"want to change"** is not strong, forget it. Stop reading, put this book on the shelf with those other books that don't make you important, they just make you look important. If your **"want to change"** is strong, read on and harness the changes that will cause you to be better at,

   ... *Closing the Sale.*

Step 2: You must, *"Change the way you think!"*

"We are generally 'Down-On' that which we are not 'Up-On'!" We need more and better information to help us change the way we think. Here's an example:

Let's consider the four-letter word, "SHIT." It's a bad word, right? Where did it come from, and who was the smart person that made putting together these four letters as something bad?

Here's how it happened: In the 16th and 17th centuries, everything had to be transported by ship and it was also before the development of commercial fertilizers, so large shipments of animal manure were quite common. The manure was dried-out to make it lighter before it was piled into the hull of the boat. On occasion water seeped into the hull and as it mixed with the manure, methane gas was created. If a member of the crew, with a lantern, entered the hull . . . BOOM! Got the picture? So, they began placing a sign on the manure. It read, "Store High in Transport"; this directive soon turned into the acronym "SHIT." Nothing wrong with that, right? Then one day some clever person decided to use this former innocuous four-letter word in his little mind-control game. He began to program his offspring from birth to believe that the word shit was a dirty word, based, no doubt, on the manure's bad smell. He taught his children that it's okay to say doo-doo, it's okay to say caca, and it's acceptable to say number two, poo and poop; but if you say shit, you'll get your mouth washed out with soap and you'll go to bed without eating.

Now that you understand more about the word's origin, don't you think it's status as a dirty word is a little stupid? Even though this information may cause you to reconsider this four-letter word, it's probably not important enough for you to have a strong desire to change the way it's used.

Comedian Buddy Hacket once asked me, *"How can you get a lovely church going old lady to say, Oh Shit? Just have another lovely church going old lady say Bingo!"*

How have you been programmed to think about that nasty four-letter word, "SALE?" Is selling a good or a bad thing to you? Do you consider yourself a "salesperson," or do you hate the idea of selling and find the word insulting? Have you ever said, "I'm not a good salesperson" or "I don't like to sell?" Do any of these phrases describe your thinking? If so, because you're involved in a profession, where you must sell to exist, doesn't it make good sense to change how you think about selling? If your answer is, "Yes!" then it's time to move on to the next step.

Step 3: You must, **"Change What You Believe!"**

You usually believe what y<u>ou</u> say, because y<u>our</u> words and thoughts are true for y<u>ou</u>. Sometimes you must fake it until you make it, and changing how you believe things should happen is rather easy if you have changed the way you think. If you think that closing the sale is important, and if you believe that closing the sale is a necessary part of the process, the next step will automatically take place.

Step 4: You must, **"Change Your Attitude!"**

I don't believe you can *start* by changing your attitude. It's only after you complete the first three steps that your positive attitude becomes real. The greater your belief, the more real your positive attitude will be. The more positive your attitude, the more your confidence will show, and you'll find it much easier to influence others to your way of thinking.

Step 5: **"Your Behavior Will Change!"**

When your attitude changes your behavior will change and when your behavior changes, you'll start getting the different results you desire, and the change is complete.

"Act the part and you'll become the part."

Dr. William James

Here are three simple rules to help with your change!

Rule-1   **Practice the art of saying something positive whenever you speak!**

There was a man in prison who was practicing saying something positive whenever he spoke. One morning, the guards came and got his cellmate. He asked, *"Where are they taking you?"* His cellmate said, *"They're taking me to the electric chair!"* To this he replied,

"More power to you!"

Rule-2   **Practice the art of hearing something positive whenever you listen!**

Two twin boys had two totally different attitudes. One was extremely positive and the other extremely negative. Their parents decided they would bring them both closer to reality on Christmas. They said to the negative boy, *"Here are your gifts!"* His gifts filled the room. The boy said, *"What a lousy day, all these toys are going to get broken, and I will be blamed!"* To the positive boy, who was practicing the art or hearing something positive whenever he listened, they said, *"Here is your gift!"* His gift was a pile of horse manure. With a slap on his fanny, he galloped off saying, *"I haven't found him yet but, I got a pony!"*

Rule-3   **Practice SIB KIS! (See It Big, but Keep It Simple)**

There was a heater salesperson making a presentation to an elderly lady. He saw it big and explained, *"This is a great heater. It's the latest model Dual Hose AC/Heater has 100,000 BTU AHRI / 7,000 BTU SACC Cooling Capacity, 11,000 BTU Heating Capacity, and 91.2 Pints/Day Dehumidification. This AC unit has two hoses; one functions as an exhaust hose and the other as an intake hose that will draw outside hot air. The air is cooled and expelled into the area. Dual-hose versions operate more quickly as it has a more efficient air exchange process and is more effective at cooling larger spaces than the single-hose variants. It has a Super Silent Self-Evaporative System, an Auto Restart Function, Refrigerant Leakage Detection, Self-Diagnosis and Auto Protection."*

To this the lady said, **"All I want to know is, will it keep me warm in the winter and cool in the summer?"**

When making a presentation, tell a story to make your point and don't tell a story unless it makes your point!

Be sure to sell benefits, not features.

There are millions of ¼ inch drill bits sold in America each year. No one wanted a ¼ inch drill bit, they wanted a ¼ inch hole!

CHAPTER TWO

Controlling Your Attitude

In 1890, Harvard University philosopher and psychologist Dr. William James said, "We can alter our lives by altering our attitudes." I paraphrase James when I say that we can alter the lives of the people whom we serve by altering their attitudes with our positive motivation.

A few years ago, on a sad day for England, a fatal automobile accident claimed the life of the beautiful, young **Princess Diana**. During the same week, the world lost one of its greatest servants, **Mother Teresa**. A third prominent person died that same week, a man I never met, but from whom I learned a profound philosophical lesson that has influenced my life in a positive way, **Dr. Viktor Frankl**.

Between 1941-1945, Nazi Germany and its collaborators systematically murdered some six million Jews, around two-thirds of

Europe's Jewish population. Shortly after surviving the Holocaust, the Jewish neurologist, Dr. Viktor Frankl authored a book entitled, *Man's Search for Meaning,* in which he described the horror of his imprisonment at Auschwitz. Prior to being sent to Auschwitz, Frankl served as head of the department of neurology at the Rothschild Hospital in Vienna. As his homeland was occupied by Germany prior to America entering World War II, Dr. Frankl had to make a difficult choice. He and his wife could leave Austria and come to America or stay in Vienna and face the consequences. The choice was easy except for one problem, if he left Austria, he could not bring his parents. A religious man, he asked God to give him a sign so he would know what to do. That day his father told him that as he passed the Synagogue which had been bombed, he found a small piece of stone from a plaque on which the "Ten Commandments" had been engraved. Victor asked of which commandment was the stone a part of and his father replied, *"Honor thy father and thy mother."* Dr. Frankl accepted this as his sign and decided to stay with his parents. The Nazis closed Rothschild Hospital. His wife Tilly died in the Bergen Belsen concentration camp. Frankl, his parents, and his brother were sent to Theresienstadt concentration camp, where his father died of starvation. Frankl, his mother, and brother were then sent to Auschwitz concentration camp. Soon after their arrival, his mother and brother were taken to the gas chamber. Stripped of all material possessions, draped in rags, his body turned to skin and bones, Frankl, on his knees, looked up into the staring eyes of the prison guard who was pulling Frankl's wedding ring from his scrawny finger. Soon he would have nothing but his remembrance of the past. In that moment of profound desperation came this thought which was equally profound. Everything could be taken from man, his possessions, his family, his health, and his freedom. What could not be taken was man's greatest freedom.

"Man's greatest freedom is that he gets to

choose his attitude with any given

set of circumstances!"

Dr. Frankl's thought is possibly the most profound philosophical lesson that I have ever learned. It influenced my life in an extremely positive way. The troubles and problems we face each day are not here to break us; they are here to make us. Show me a person who accepts their problems as challenges and solves them daily and I'll show you a person on the road to a successful lifestyle. And irrespective of what negative events we might encounter we get to choose our attitude. A positive attitude begets a positive existence, and your attitude is more contagious than the flu.

We have the power to change how we think on any given subject. Just imagine you have worked all day, and you are worn out. You are going to take a bus ride home. You have saved today's paper so you can relax on the bus and read it. You are reading the paper when the bus stops at a corner and a man gets on with his six young kids. As the bus moves on, you continue reading when suddenly, Bam! A kid smacks the back of your paper, and you jump in the air. You then approach the man and in an angry voice holler, "Can't you see what's going on! Your unruly kids are all over the bus making everyone miserable." The man looks up with watery eyes and says, *"I'm so sorry, we just came from the hospital. My wife, the kids mother just died and I guess I'm not handling it very well, I'm very sorry!"* Might your attitude now change, and might you now begin to play with the children?

When as a kid, I went out to play, the first task was to build a toy. I made slingshots, willow whistles, darts, kites, and wagons. If I could find an old barrel, I would break it apart, and I had a toy that would keep me busy for hours. Using one of the wooden slats, I would hit one of the round metal barrel binding hoops to start it rolling. While I could bounce the metal hoop up and down, one thing for sure, the direction in which I hit it was the only direction the hoop went. It never went two directions at the same time. On a negative, down slope the hoop would often pick up momentum and I had difficulty keeping up.

Years later while instructing a class at a success seminar, speaking about attitude, I used my childhood toy as a metaphor. I commented that the human mind moves either in a positive or negative direction, and while sometimes in the morning, it may bounce up and down, it never goes in both directions at the same time. And like the barrel hoop, once the mind gets rolling especially in a negative direction, it's overwhelming and keeping up becomes difficult. Unfortunately, what most people don't realize is that they hold the slat and can give their thinking a whack in the right direction. To replace the slat, I wrote a poem which I had printed on my coffee cup and say it out loud every morning. I gave a cup to my friend, Art Linkletter, who had written "Kids say the darndest things!" Art co-authored a book with Mark Hanson who wrote, "Chicken Soup for the soul." They took a line out of my poem and named their book, "How to make the rest of your life the best of your life!" My poem is simple, and it goes like this.

Today!

Today is going to be a great day;

because I am going to make it that way.

And the rest of my life shall be the best of my life;

because today is going to be a great day!

Attitude is contagious! A professional salesperson was a little late as he headed to his place of business. He heard a siren and then saw a patrol officer in his rear-view mirror. After receiving his ticket, he said to the officer, *"Why aren't you out arresting bad guys instead of good tax paying citizens like me?"* **Boy, he was mad!** When he arrived at his place of business his office secretary said, *"You were late, and your appointment left."* He then said in an angry voice, *"What do I pay you for, it's your job to keep them here!"* He went into his office and slammed the door. **Boy, was his secretary mad!** To herself she said, *"I've been working here for ten years, and I do everything for everyone and get no thanks. Why should he blame me when he was the one who was late!"* She walked out and went home. When she got home, she found her eight-year-old son lying on the floor watching TV, eating a sandwich. She grabbed him up by his shirt collar and sent him towards his room as she said, *"I've been working hard all day and all you do is watch TV, get in there and do your homework!"* **Boy, that made him mad,** and he said, *"I've been working hard at school all day, I take a break to eat and watch my favorite show and I get treated like this!"* About then the cat walked in front of him, and he kicked the cat halfway across the room. Now I ask you, *"Why didn't the salesperson go directly to the secretary's home and kick the cat himself?"*

CHAPTER THREE

Third -Party Influence

"The prospect may be the head of the house,

But don't forget the importance of the spouse.

The head will make the decision, or so it is said.

The spouse is the neck, and the neck turns the head."

No matter what product or service you are selling, or for what price you are selling it, the spouse or other third-party may have a tremendous influence on, or even be in total control of, the buying decision. If your product or service sells for hundreds or thousands of dollars, the decision usually comes after receiving the approval or at least the acceptance of a wife, husband, friend, or business associate. If the influencing person is not present during your presentation, odds are it will end with; "I need to talk it over with _____, and I'll call you back later." Your prospect becomes the interpreter between you and the influential third-party, and the third-party never receives the presentation the way you would present it. Here is the story in point.

The mafia had a problem with their bagman who collected their money. If the bagman got caught, they would talk too much. The mafia found what they thought was the perfect solution. They hired a deaf-mute. They felt if he got caught, he could not talk. The deaf-mute did his job very well until one day the boss found a million dollars was missing. The boss and a sign language interpreter paid a visit to the deaf-mute. The boss said, "Ask him where my money is." The question was signed out to the deaf-mute and the answer was signed back, "I have no idea." The boss then placed his cocked pistol against the deaf mute's head and said, "Tell him if he doesn't tell me where my money is, I'm going to blow his f*cking brains all over the room." The message was given, and the deaf-mute signed back "It's in the hole in the big tree in the backyard." And the interpreter said to the boss, "He said he's not telling you and he doesn't think you've got the guts to pull the trigger."

. . . Bang!

The interpreter will tell the story differently than you would tell it. That is why most seasoned salespeople know, more often than not, the one thing a call back won't do is call back. If someone other than you is setting your presentation appointments, make sure they understand the importance of the third-party. No matter how competent a salesperson you are, your closing rate will be affected by not having the power of purchase present for your presentation.

It's up to you to decide if the decision to purchase your product or service usually needs acceptance of a third-party. If it's a lifesaving surgery, it could take the whole family. If the prospective buyer is about to purchase a new family car or a new home, the third-party influence would generally be of utmost importance. Giving your great presentation without the power of purchase present may not only waste your time, but it may also ruin your only chance to,

   . . . Close the Sale!

CHAPTER FOUR

Establishing Rapport

Establishing a friendly professional relationship with the prospective buyer and the third-party is key to solving a problem and closing the sale.

> *"Your Prospective buyer and their*
> *third-party must buy you before*
> *they will buy from you!"*

According to a study conducted by the New York Sales and Marketing Club, 71% of the people who buy that which you are selling, do so because they like and trust you, the salesperson. The best way to appear as a friend is to become a friend. When you develop a friendship with a prospective buyer, closing the sale becomes rather easy. To the prospective buyer, liking and trusting the salesperson can be the single-most important factor in his or her decision to buy from you, more important than all the certificates hanging on your wall. Strong prospective buyer-salesperson relationships are more important than your technical knowledge or your large, extensive technical vocabulary.

No closing technique works unless it's built on a strong, "I like and trust you" foundation. If a prospective buyer or his or her third-party doesn't like you, doesn't trust you or doesn't feel comfortable with you, then it doesn't matter what closing technique you use—the prospective buyer will not buy from you.

Many years ago, I was operating a retail hearing instrument office in Riverside, California. On occasion, an unhappy patient who was recently delivered new hearing aids would come to my office with their hearing aids in a Ziploc bag. One of the dispensers in my office had made the sale and the delivery, and I had never met the patient. It was obvious that this was a return in the making.

After saying hello, I would place their bag of hearing instruments on the desk and then ask them to please follow me. I would then lead them out the front door and over to the little restaurant next door. They would often ask me where we were going and I would explain, "I can see you are not wearing your hearing aids and you are having a problem you wish to discuss with me. I have always found that solving a problem is much easier when people are better acquainted. So, let's have a cup of coffee and get to know each other and then we will go back to the office and solve the problem. Wouldn't knowing the person who owns the office make solving the problem a little easier? You wouldn't mind getting to know me, would you?"

Once the patient and their third-party became comfortable with me, their new friend, it was not as difficult for me to encourage them to try a little harder to solve their hearing problem. A great number of sales were saved in that little restaurant. Bottom line:

"Sell yourself, and your staff, and . . .

make sure the buyer likes and trusts you!"

Over the years I have found that this little conversation opener has helped me later when I . . . *Close the Sale.*

Memorize these seven lines; they will help build a trusting relationship with your new prospective buyer.

"Before we get started, let me tell you what I'm going to do—or better yet, let me tell you what I'm not going to do. It is not my job to make decisions for you. You are old enough and certainly smart enough to make your own decisions. It is my job to give you information so you will be able to make a good decision. Does that make sense to you?"

Once the prospective buyer and their third-party trusts that you won't try to sell them something they don't need or they can't afford, that you trust in them to make their own decision based on the information you give them, they will feel more relaxed and open to your presentation.

Actions speak louder than words!

Watch what you're saying when you're not talking. If the prospective buyer comes to your office or store, the presentation begins the second he or she enters. The appearance of your place of business often determines how the person perceives you, the salesperson. You could be placed on a pedestal or be rejected, based solely upon the décor or organization of your waiting room. Today is a good day to get your house in order. If you do your selling in the home the same is true. Your appearance matters.

First Impressions Count

If the prospective buyer and the third-party comes to your place of business. Grab a notepad, gather all the members of your staff, and go outside. Ask each staff member to look at your place of business with the eyes of a prospective buyer and the third-party. Each staff member should record his or her thoughts on the notepad. Are your business signs easy to read and understandable? Check out the paint — is it appealing or just peeling? If you have a display window, is it clean? I have seen glass business doors with so many unread, useless decals that it looked like the door of a very well-traveled camper. If your place of business has a good appearance, look to see if the neighborhood may have collapsed around you. Maybe it is time to pack up your business and move to a nicer neighborhood. As you enter your place of business, look around. What do you see? Are the desks neat and uncluttered, or are they a mess, which suggests a person with sloppy habits? Is the reading material in your waiting room of interest to a large population of your buyers? Is your reading material up to date, or do you expect your new friends to enjoy last year's magazines? If your magazines are not up to date, I suggest you have them be really old. Go to an old bookstore and purchase magazines from 20 or 30 years ago. People love to look through old magazines.

Someone once said, *"If these walls could talk."* Well, they can, and they do, and they are talking about *you*. Are the pictures on your walls fresh and new or old and dusty? Make sure that your walls give a pleasant, warm, friendly message. Also remember that the walls in the restroom speak to a captive audience. A clean and tidy restroom is a must.

How about offering a hot cup of coffee, or a cold bottle of water? An awake, comfortable buyer is better than a sleepy one. Being sleepy or thirsty are good reasons for the prospective buyer to leave before you have finished closing the sale.

So far you haven't said a word, but your prospective buyer has heard volumes. In fact, he and his third-party have already made many important decisions about you, based solely on your appearance and the physical condition of your place of business. My wife won't eat in a restaurant if the windows are dirty. You may find that your buyer and his or her third-party reflect their perceptions in the objections they raise during your presentation. If prospective buyers are not pleased with their first impressions, which you have only one opportunity to make, they will probably decide to shop around.

The Parent-Child Relationship

When communicating with your prospect, it is necessary to select words that are easy to understand. The *Wall Street Journal*, written at an eighth grade reading level, is a great example of how to communicate with a broad audience. Two small words are better than one big word. If you use the technical jargon of your profession and not the language of your prospective buyers, who are real people with varying levels of education, the prospective buyers may not understand a word you are saying. If they don't understand you, they won't buy from you.

Human influence is the result of the words you choose, your manner of speech and your body language. Your vocabulary accounts for only 7% of human influence; tonality, volume and tempo comprise 38%; and body language, gestures, posture, and energy are responsible for 54% of your total ability to influence another person.

"If your verbalization is not congruent with what your body language is saying, your prospective buyer will believe your body language and disbelieve your verbal language."

As you speak, one of three communicative relationships quickly develops: parent-to-child, child-to-parent, or adult-to-adult. A child to parent relationship, with you as the child and the prospective buyer as the parent, might be good at the reception counter, where it is important for you to appear flexible and yielding; however, if you are the child counseling the parent, you give your prospective buyer the position of strength. The objections of the parent will be stronger, perhaps impossible for you, the child, to overcome. Adult-to-adult relationships often result in debating and seldom work in any professional situation. No one is in charge; decisions are not made, and nothing is accomplished. An adult-to-adult relationship usually ends without agreement and leads to an "I'll think it over" or an "I'm going to wait a while." Many successful doctors model their doctor-to-patient relationships after the patent-to-child relationship. In the parent role, you are in the position of compassionate strength. The child has a need or want for help from the parent. After careful analysis, the parent offers a solution. The child's objections are usually weaker and easier to overcome. If you act the part of the parent, your prospective buyer, irrespective of age or social status, will usually assume the child's position in your relationship. Because of your training, experience, and product knowledge, you deserve to be the parent in the parent-to-child relationship.

You can move toward the parent role with the use of a few physical actions that will work most of the time. Have you ever heard the expression, "You can't trust him—he won't look you in the eye." Winning the battle of eye contact is important and easy. It's the old grade-school stare-down. When you first face your prospective buyer and their third-party, look directly into their eyes until they look away. Being unaware of the contest, your prospective buyer and their third-party will generally look away within a second or two. Remember:

"The will that weakens first,

strengthens the other."

Although they will probably not realize they have "lost" this contest of wills, your prospective buyer and his or her third-party will slip into the position of "child," unconsciously perceiving you as the "parent" or authority figure within the context of this exchange. Practice this technique with the next few people you meet. Look them in the eye until they turn away. They will subconsciously know that they have lost the position of strength and allow you to take the dominant role. The next time you stop at a red light and catch eye contact with the driver of an adjacent car, don't look away. It may surprise you that it is often difficult to make this contact, and it will require willpower to establish this position in a relationship. I'm not suggesting that you constantly stare at your prospective buyer and third-party, just win the first "battle," and you will have established your respective roles. As your presentation progresses, closing will come easier, and objections will be softened because your prospective buyer will feel you are stronger and will follow your recommendations.

Another technique you can use to establish yourself as the authority is to elevate yourself so that you are seated a little higher than your prospective buyer and their third-party. Never sit with a desk between you and them. Make sure you can reach out and touch the prospective buyer, being careful to touch appropriately.

No matter if they are patients, clients, or customers . . . If you want your prospective buyer to perceive you as a professional, it is important to look like, act and speak like a professional.

Imagine for a minute that you are sitting in a restaurant. You notice a young man leaving his table. As he leaves, he says, "I have to hurry, I have a patient waiting." As you turn and glance out the window, you see three vehicles: a Ford pick-up, a Chevy van, and a Mercedes sedan. Which vehicle do you think is his? Do you think he is educated? Is he successful? Is he a person you would like to know? Consider your answers. They all came as a response to hearing the word "patient." Your prospective buyer may be a patient, a client, or a customer, make them a friend. Use their first name! Don't become hung up by your own childhood programming. Your parents may have told you to show respect for others by using surnames, but a lot of what we were taught as children doesn't work well in the marketplace. More than any other reason, people buy from a person they like and trust. The best way to be seen and be treated as a friend is to do as friends do and develop enough conversational intimacy with your prospective buyer that it becomes appropriate to refer to them by their first names. Act the part, and you become the part. People like and trust their friends, and friends call each other by their first names. Getting from surname to first name takes a little tact. You may ask, "What do your friends call you?" When your prospective buyer tells you, ask if you may call them by that name, as well. If you ask with a smile, you will almost certainly hear a "yes." Some readers might think that calling their prospective buyer by their first name seems unprofessional and might feel uncomfortable about making this change. Remember: You may be doing that which makes you *look* important instead of doing that which will make you important. You could be professionalizing yourself to death.

"If you continue to think as you have always thought, you'll continue to get what you've always got."

What would you do in this situation?

You are driving on a very stormy night when you come to a bus stop, where there are three people waiting for the bus. One is a sick elderly lady, who is going to die if she doesn't get immediately to the hospital. Next is an old friend, who once saved your life and will lose his life's savings if he does not make it to his meeting on time. Last is your dream partner for life, about whom you have been dreaming about for years. Knowing that there could only be one passenger in your car, to which person would you offer a ride? Stop and think before you continue reading. This is a moral/ethical dilemma that was once used as part of a job application. You could choose the elderly woman and save her life. You could choose your old friend, save his life's savings, and repay him for his great deed helping you in the past. On the other hand, if you miss this opportunity, you may never again find the mate of your dreams.

The candidate who was hired answered, *"I would give my car keys to my friend and have him drop the elderly lady at the hospital on his way to his meeting. Meanwhile, I would hang out waiting for the bus with the mate of my dreams."* Sometimes we gain a great deal by giving up the stubborn thoughts that limit our progress. It is hard to change what you have come to believe but, at least, give new thoughts a chance and remember once again,

"Change is the price we must pay for progress."

CHAPTER FIVE

Your Presentation

"Selling Is a Process of Education"

Y ou say you excel in the technical aspects of your profession, but you just don't like selling? Maybe you think the traits of a salesperson are congenital. Some believe a successful salesperson must be a "born salesperson", with a dynamic, extroverted personality. Think about this, what's more important, the gift of gab or the ability to listen?

"We are what we repeatedly do.

Excellence, then, is not an act, but a habit."

Aristotle

It is your presentation that leads to the successful sale. While an outgoing, extroverted personality may be an asset, it is not a necessity. Honesty, integrity, and a sincere desire to help others are a few characteristics that are necessary to become a successful salesperson in any profession. To appear sincere, one must *be* sincere; to appear competent, one must *be* competent. No matter how smart or educated you are, no matter what a great talker or listener you may be, remember:

"People want to know how much you care before they care how much you know."

If you sell that which people need, yes, you will make sales, but if you are *only* selling that which people need, the objections you will receive will be numerous and your negotiated prices will probably be low. You will accomplish a great deal more if you sell that which people want!

"Successful Closing happens when preparation meets opportunity!"

Selling is a negotiation, and often, it's a negotiation the unprepared salesperson will lose. The purpose of the presentation is first to educate, and then to motivate. We must educate the prospective buyer and those people who influence them. Once we establish beyond question that the need exists, we must then motivate the prospective buyer into acting.

You will find that I will often repeat those things I believe are important because repetition causes us to remember. I recommend that you repeat the elements of your presentation for the same reason.

And so, to repeat, at the beginning of a presentation, say:

"Before we get started, let me tell you what I'm going to do — or better yet, let me tell you what I'm not going to do. It is not my job to make decisions for you. You are old enough and certainly smart enough to make your own decisions. It is my job to give you information so you will be able to make good decisions. Does that make sense to you?"

"To sell the buyer, what the buyer buys, you must see the buyer, through the buyer's eyes."

In other words, you must know what makes the buyer tick and what makes them ticked! Be a friend and never become over aggressive.

I'm not a psychologist. I do know, however, about the behavioral traits of the prospective buyer. The two most prominent traits are suspicion and indecision. I have made this observation from working with prospective buyers for over 60 years and from my own experiences as a buyer. I have dealt with the buyer traits from both an objective and subjective perspective. Your job is to overcome the suspicion and gently persuade the prospective buyer to make the decision.

As a comparison, I offer you the example of a court of law. Would you not agree that the jury exhibits these same two characteristics, suspicion, and indecisiveness? Are they not suspicious of the lawyers? Aren't both the plaintiff and the defendant suspect? Of course, all witnesses will be questioned. Then the jurors are directed by the judge, maybe the only person in the courtroom they trust, not to predetermine the case; in other words, the judge instructs them to remain indecisive. The lawyer, during his or her presentation, must remove suspicion and guide the jury into making the right decision. Based on how it is presented, the evidence will determine the jury's decision.

In court the lawyer cannot lead the witness, this is not true in your presentation. If you ask the right questions, you will get the right answers.

During our presentation we must clearly and concisely remove all suspicion, and then, without causing a feeling of pressure, guide the buyer into making the right decision. Does that seem logical to you?

Unfortunately, I don't know if you are a neophyte or a seasoned veteran. If you are an experienced salesperson, I would like you to answer this question:

"What is the most difficult buyer objection

for you to overcome?"

Perhaps it is a "money objection", or maybe the prospective buyer might need to "think it over", or maybe your prospective buyer doesn't believe their need is bad enough to pay the price of your solution? Whichever objection you think is the most difficult to overcome *is* the most difficult objection for you to overcome. It is what I call your "rut" objection, and you are probably pretty good at overcoming it. Your presentation leads you into this rut, so you get lots of practice trying to talk your way out of it. Here is an interesting question: Why is it that all salespeople don't all share the same rut objection? Could it be that objections come because of our presentation strategy? Do you create the objection you must then overcome?

Let me compare your presentation to a path down a mountain which you will lead your prospective buyer. Although you may have traveled down this path hundreds of times, your prospective buyer has never been here before. You are an experienced guide taking the buyer where he or she has never been. If your path leads the prospective buyer to the edge of a cliff called indecision, are you not responsible? If you keep falling in the same rut, over and over, don't you think it's time to take a different path? Albert Einstein described insanity as when we keep doing something over and over in the same way and somehow expect to get different results.

Don't allow yourself to fall prey to this form of insanity in your presentation.

Nothing presented in this book is theory. I have used every idea thousands of times over the past 60 years. These ideas have been modified and improved, and I guarantee they will work for you. It is important that you design a presentation that fits the product or service you are selling and follow your presentation, adjusting from time to time to overcome objections _before_ they come up. Allow me to say that again,

"Overcome objections <u>before</u> they come up!"

CHAPTER SIX

Overcoming Objections and Closing the Sale

"Consider overcoming objections to be a psychological rock fight. The objections are the rocks, and you are wise to let the prospective buyer throw his or her rocks first."

Can you believe it? After you have given your fantastic presentation, instead of giving you their credit card and having you write-up the sale, the prospective buyer gives you a reason why he or she can't purchase your product or service. What happened? The prospective buyer and the third-party are intelligent people, and yet, they're still indecisive. What went wrong? Nothing happened. Nothing went wrong. Objections are not bad. Objections are nothing more than questions waiting to be answered. Objection handling is a very common part of the sales process. The onus lies on you, the salesperson to overcome these objections, alleviate the prospective buyers' concerns, build trust, and then,

. . . Close the Sale!

I asked you earlier to think of the hardest objection for you to overcome, and here is the answer: Because it is impossible to overcome an objection about which you do not know,

> **"The hardest objection to overcome is the one they don't tell you."**

You must listen very carefully to the objection they give and make sure it's the true objection. The spoken objection often masks the true, unspoken issues that lie under the surface. Uncover the true objection by asking questions such as, *"If money were no object, what would be your ideal solution?"* If you and the prospective buyer can achieve a common goal, it'll be easier to work out other issues. Active listening can not only aid you in understanding the true objection, which is the most important step to successfully overcome it; you will lessen the objection by listening and gain an understanding of the objection that will help you respond sincerely and make the prospective buyer feel you have heard their concerns. Understanding their hesitance to decide to purchase also informs how you can convince them to purchase.

If the prospective buyer asks a question in the form of an objection, you must answer it and then, motivate him or her to purchase. If you answer the objection and **just sit there**, you'll get another objection. So always follow your answer with a closing question such as,

Does that make sense to you? If the answer is, "Yes!"

. . . *Close the Sale!*

Overcoming objections takes a logical explanation and emotional motivation. Using logic is great to educate the prospective buyer to their needs. When you use logic only, you'll often fail to close the sale. If you only give logical answers, you will make a lot of sales for your competitors.

If you use emotion only, you will sell a lot and get a lot of cancellations. If a prospective buyer buys because they got excited, when they get home, they won't know why they bought and may call back and cancel.

Here is an example of the easy-to-understand logic I used when selling better hearing.

"Our five senses are synergistic in that they work together, like how five musical instruments complement each other in a band. When all your five senses are in tune it creates a sixth sense and you accomplish a great deal automatically almost without thought, like driving a car. Sometimes you get places without thinking. The problem begins when all instruments remain in the band, but one instrument is played off-key. If a person loses one sense, the other four may become more keenly focused to compensate for the loss. Like the band, the problem begins when all senses remain, but one functions poorly. For example, if a person spills his or her coffee while setting down the cup, you may think that person is clumsy. You would not blame a loss of hearing. However, if the person didn't hear the little 'click' as the cup touched the saucer, he or she may have let go of the cup too soon. Hearing often signals other reactions. If the signal is not heard, the reaction may be incorrect. When the phone rings, we don't wonder what it is. Our hand automatically picks up the handset and places it over our ear, and we say, "Hello." It is the sound we heard that triggered the other responses. We feed our body through our mouth; we feed our mind through our senses. When the senses grow dim, the mind grows dim. After gaining attention with an interesting story, you answer their objection directly and then say, *"Let's keep your senses sharp"* and,

. . . Close the Sale!

Recently my wife Jean and I went out to buy a new electric stove top. At the first appliance store the salesperson after showing us several different products, seemed disinterested and told us he would email us information so we can find what we are looking for. He appeared too busy to spend the time with us. We left and went to the next store. The lady who greeted us said, *"Allow me to introduce you to our expert and he will help you."* The expert was very friendly and had a lot of product knowledge. Within a short time, my wife selected a stove top featuring induction heating. We left the store and were headed home when I asked, *"Since you found what you wanted, why didn't we buy it?"* She replied, *"We should have, let's go back and buy it!"* We went back and found the salesperson and told him we wanted to buy the stove top he had shown us. He then instructed us to go home and place a magnet on the bottom of each of our pots and pans to make sure they would accept the induction system. The salesperson could have and should have closed the sale. The difference between a salesperson and a (PR) public relations person is the PR person sells the product or service but doesn't close the sale. We went to a third store knowing what we wanted and bought it.

Anticipate and prepare to address the objection. Objections can be a good thing. When you get an objection, it shows your prospective buyer wants to move forward, but something bothers them. Address and answer the objection and,

. . . Close the Sale.

Closing is an art form. In golf it is said:

"You drive for the show...You PUTT for the dough!"

In the sales profession, we say:

"You present for the show...You CLOSE for the dough!"

Closing is a make-or-break moment in sales. When you use the right phrases and techniques, you will,

. . . Close the Sale!

Success in closing a sale wouldn't be so thrilling without high emotional stakes, like fear of failure and rejection.

My favorite part about closing sales is that each single scenario that'll ever happen is different. That's why salespeople struggle the most with overcoming objections and ultimately closing the sale. There's no one single way to do it. I recommend you have an arsenal of closing techniques along with continually practicing overcoming those objections. First things first, be sure to clearly define the prospective buyer's needs that your product or service is intended to solve. Your presentation must explain your product or service's benefits. Once again, don't sell features, sell benefits. Be sure to create a sense of urgency. Urgency creates a reason for your prospective buyer to move forward _now_!

Your product could be a great fit for your prospective buyer. It's within their budget, you've offered them the perfect discount, it should be a slam dunk. But unless they feel a sense of urgency, they may, "put-it-off."

You can create urgency by offering a time-limited discount. And remember, there's a thin line between creating a sense of urgency and appearing to be high pressure. Crossing that line could make you miss the sale altogether.

Most salespeople I've met regard "the close" as the most difficult part of the sales process. I disagree; I believe it should be the simplest. If you have done everything properly then closing the sale is just a formality. And remember, closing the sale starts long before you approach it. The prospective buyer and the third-party have made several decisions about you and your place of business which will affect your ability to close before they meet you. If prospective buyers aren't pleased with their first impressions, if their initial decisions are negative, closing the sale will be more difficult and maybe impossible.

Several *decisions* were made when they called to make their appointment. They *decided* if your staff is friendly. They *decided* if the instructions on how to find you were easy to understand and follow. They *decided* they liked or didn't like your parking. They *decided* if the outside appearance of your office was clean and well kept. They *decided* that the decor of your office was or was not pleasing. They *decided* they liked or disliked how they were greeted. They *decided* they liked or disliked your choice of reading material. They *decided* they were pleased when they were offered a hot cup of coffee, or a bottle of water.

The following few chapters will analyze some common objections and techniques to close the sale. Your task is to tailor each close to fit your product or service. Find the close that fits you best!

CHAPTER SEVEN

The Money Objection

C onsidered the hardest objection to overcome by many, the money objection is sometimes difficult because of our early programming. As stated earlier, our parents may have taught us as children not to ask for money; not very good training when we end up living in a society in which money is used to keep score and working in a profession in which our success depends to some degree on our ability to ask for and get the money!

The money objection must be understood before you attempt to overcome it. What is the prospective buyer really saying? *" I don't have that much money. Your product or service is too expensive. I believe I can buy it for less from your competitor."*

The money objection is common. However, you can overcome almost any price objection, get your full fees, and avoid discounting.

If you lower your price, it is important to give a reason that makes sense for lowering it. Being arbitrary creates distrust. Review the parts of your solution and ask, *"What part don't you want?"* This leads to either a reduction in scope or having the prospective buyer realize the whole package is the best solution. By understanding the common types of sales objections, you can recognize the true issues sooner. This will allow you to quickly apply a strategy to understand, address, discuss and ultimately overcome objections which will allow you to close the sale sooner.

"An objection is not a rejection; it is simply a request for more information."

Make sure you are listening and providing that information and not just rushing to the close.

The prospective buyer may say, "I can get it cheaper."

Well, it's difficult to argue with that logic if your product or service appears very similar to another product or service, but costs more. But is that usually the case? No! If it was, you wouldn't be in business for very long. With this objection, you need to convince your prospective buyer that cheaper isn't always better. Show them exactly why your product or service costs more and show them why it's better. Demonstrate how some of your advanced features that they would be paying for will help them, and you'll be in a better position to overcome the objection.

Determining just what the prospective buyer is saying can be difficult because the money objection is often a smokescreen used to camouflage the true reason for not buying. The prospective buyer drives up to your place of business in a new Mercedes, is well-dressed and dripping in jewelry, and then claims not to be able to afford the product or service he came to buy. Be careful not to judge the book by its often-understated cover. The fact that the prospective buyer is poorly dressed in outdated clothing may only describe lifestyle and not financial capability.

When you are given the money objection, the prospective buyer is saying, *"I want to buy your product. I just can't or won't spend the money."* I like to explain to the prospective buyer that there is no better place to spend his or her money than on his or herself. As a matter of fact, when a buyer spends money on him or herself, he or she is not really lessening what he or she has but changing it from money to something of more use.

Anyone can give their products away. It takes skill to sell them. Always start with the assumption that the prospective buyer can afford the best. Make your first offer based on the best solution for the prospective buyer's need, and then analyze the response. If you determine that the prospective buyer is being sincere and really cannot afford that which you have offered, change the offer, and use . . .

The Finance Close

The Finance Close can only be used if financing is available. In that case, the closing question may be. *"Can you afford $106 per month?"* People who always buy on time seem to be more concerned with the amount of the monthly payment than they are with the price of the product. The decision to purchase is based on how much they can afford to pay per month.

You might say, *"If we put this on your credit card, we will pay the interest for one year."* Six percent of a $3,000 balance is a $180 discount.

"That way, you get all the benefits of paying cash without the outlay of money today. The good news is that you can enjoy the benefits of the product or service right away. Does that make sense to you?" If they say yes,

. . . Close the Sale!

If you feel the prospect has the money but thinks your product costs too much, consider using the,

The Inducement Close

Everyone likes to make a good deal and save money, especially seniors, who have been negotiating for years. We all love to get something of value at a better-than-usual price. It's the American way of selling. It's the American way of buying. Companies that have earned your respect because you believe they are ethical and maintain a high standard of integrity have great sales: Neiman Marcus, Nordstrom, and others. They must start by setting their prices high enough to accommodate a discount, and still make a profit.

The Inducement close is one of the best ways to encourage the prospective buyer to act now. You might say, *"If we go ahead with this today, our company has a special 'one appointment' discount. When we finish this transaction in one appointment instead of two or more, we save time and you save money, 10%. Do you like saving money?"* A Yes answer to the easy question is a Yes decision.

The Inducement Close may also be used to encourage a cash-with-the-order purchase. Be careful when offering a cash discount. Seniors especially are great negotiators; they've had a lot of practice. Once they realize that your price is flexible, they may want more. If you do give a cash discount, be sure to give a reason that makes sense.

If you determine that the prospect believes he can purchase the same product elsewhere cheaper, use the,

The Most Important Decision Close

The "Most Important Decision" close can be used when the decision seems to be on the fence and could go either way.

You say: *"The most important decision you must make, related to your need, is your choice of who is going to be the person to help you. If you choose the right person, the odds of success are great. What I look for with my buyers is a long-term relationship. Your service needs will not go away, so I'm probably going to be in your life for the rest of your life. If I do a good job for you, we will become good friends. Do you think you could stand having me as a friend?"* If the answer to this easy question is Yes, then you say, *"let's get started."* And,

. . . ***Close the Sale!***

REMEMBER: Don't turn a statement such as, *"WOW! These things are expensive,"* into an objection to be overcome. Respond to a statement with a statement, *"Yes, everything is too expensive these days. I can remember when gas was 19 cents a gallon, but that's the way life is."* Then use the,

The Sir Isaac Newton Close

The "Sir Isaac Newton" close starts with the forming of an attitude. You must believe that the prospective buyer has come to you to have his or her need or want fulfilled. A good question to ask in the beginning of your presentation is, *"How may I help you?"* The answer to this simple question will help you to decide your course of action. If, for example, the prospective buyer says, *"I have a need and I need to solve it,"* or *"I would like your opinion about my problem,"* you assume that if a need exists, the prospective buyer wants to correct it. You then allow this assumption to dominate your approach and the prospective buyer's actions. **"A body in motion will stay in motion,"** and if the prospective buyer decides not to proceed, he or she must stop the process with an objection. Assuming consent keeps you from manufacturing objections that may not exist. Assuming buying consent keeps you from turning comments and questions into objections that may not exist.

Why the "Sir Isaac Newton" close works.

When you assume consent, it gives two choices to the prospective buyer, he or she believes you or they distrust you. If your presentation was successful, they're more likely to believe you. When one person acts confidently as if something is true, it is hard for others to deny it. Assuming consent prevents the prospective buyer from thinking about the reasons why they should not get your product or service.

The best time to use this sales closing technique.

If you believe that your product or service is exactly what the prospective buyer is looking for, you can apply this closing technique. As stated, this technique has started way before you become ready to close because you began your presentation simply assuming the person in front of you will buy your service or product. All you do is deliver a successful presentation and let your prospective buyer realize you are assuming he or she will purchase in the end. It works by the salesperson assuming the prospective buyer is ready to buy. But instead of simply saying, *"Are you ready to buy?"*, you instead assume the sale by asking assumptive closing questions like, *"Would you like me to arrange for delivery on Monday or Tuesday?"*

However, like any other sales closing technique, there are right ways and not-so-right ways to make use of the assumptive close. One key to success in this technique involves making a seamless transition between your presentation and the Sir Isaac Newton Close.

Action is a necessary part of the closing process. When it's time to close, you simply ask a closing question like, *"In what name would you like this written up?"*

A few other closing questions: *"When should we get started on implementation?* or *"To whose name should I make the invoice?* or *"Do you want the upgrade with this, also? And,*

  . . . Close the Sale.

If you believe the money objection is just a smokescreen; you may want to use the,

The Easy Question Close

It is often easier to answer a simple, easy question than it is to make a big decision. Instead of asking a direct question, such as, *"Would you like to buy my product or service?"* ask an easy to answer question: *"Would you enjoy the benefits of my product or service?"* Another example might come after explaining the necessary steps to proceed:

"So what we need to do to get started now is to fill out this form which will only take about 5 minutes. It will take about a week to get your product and then I will come and deliver it to you. Does that make sense to you?"

If the buyer answers *"yes"* to either of these easy questions, then he or she has, at the same time, given consent to the direct question. A couple more examples of easy questions are: *"How do you folks usually pay for things like this?"* and *"Would a morning appointment be best for your delivery, or would you prefer an afternoon appointment?"* Always give them a choice between something and something, not something and nothing.

The positive response to these questions signals consent.

. . . ***Close the Sale!***

CHAPTER EIGHT

Anchoring!

During my career as a Hearing Aid Specialist, I spent many years as, "A Visiting Expert" in hearing aid offices across the country. I would work three days a week on a Special Promotion in which I counseled an average of 100 patients. The presentation was conducted by the resident dispenser and then I would be called in. I would see each patient for about fifteen minutes and my job was to,

. . . Close the Sale!

I worked in this capacity for over five years. In those five years I attempted to close the sale somewhere around twenty-five thousand times. Because of the limited time I spent with each patient, I created a system of closing that worked over 90% of the time based on Anchoring. It takes a little effort to set up but, I believe this system will work for you regardless of your product or service. Here is how it works:

When I ask salespeople when they tell the prospective buyer the price, their usual answer is, "At the END of my presentation". And... the prospective buyer almost always has a total misconception about how much your product and services cost. We asked several salespeople to analyze the product prices quoted in their local newspaper ads, the Internet and TV ads. But don't be misled—the prospective buyer has come to see you with intent to purchase your product and solve their need. Especially men! Men are not shoppers, men are buyers.

The prospective buyer meets you. You dress and look the way they expect a professional to dress and look. You speak the way they expect a professional to speak; you act the way they expect a professional to act. This is true because you are a professional.

As a professional, you know that your first task is to establish a friendly, positive rapport. You then make a great impression when you give your well-planned presentation.

He or she wants what you are selling, the buying signs are strong, and when you reveal the price, the prospective buyer's mind goes blank, and the stuttering begins. That's when you hear, "I must think it over" or "I want to sleep on it." You have used up all your good reasons why the buyer should purchase, and you now must start overcoming objections. No matter how smooth you are at overcoming objections, your professionalism wanes, and you start sounding like you are applying pressure. And all too often the sale is lost. After doing so many things right, you failed to motivate the buyer to purchase. What happened? The prospective buyer came to your office to buy and somehow you sold them out of it. How did you miss this one? What did you do wrong?

"Whenever the price of your product or service is greater than the buyer's expectation, they will experience

... Sticker Shock!"

Have you not experienced sticker shock yourself in recent days? Maybe you ordered a hamburger and was handed the check for $15.50. What about the last time you filled your car with gas and paid over $5.00 a gallon? The reason you may <u>not</u> have felt sticker shock at the gas pump is because you have been conditioned by the news media, which keeps telling us oil is $106 per barrel, even though most of us have never bought a barrel of oil. The media has programmed us to expect to pay $5.00 a gallon at the pump. They tell us we're lucky because gas in Europe is at $6 or $7 a gallon, and in Norway it's close to $10 a gallon. So, you go to the gas station expecting to pay $5.00 a gallon. You pay and go on your way, not thinking much about it. Matter of curiosity, if you could find gas for $2.00 a gallon, wouldn't you feel like you were stealing?

Behavioral Economic Scientists at many major universities have studied the human mind to discover the guidance system used to determine if the price of a product is reasonable. Their findings confirm that money matters mess with our mind's financial guidance systems. When we don't have a feel for what a product should cost, our brains search for a reference point. The reference point becomes the *anchor* from which we determine if the price we are about to pay is reasonable or not. If an anchor cannot be found, or if the anchor is considerably lower than the product's asking price, we become confused and in that confused state of mind . . . *we won't make a decision.*

When buying or selling an automobile, the Blue Book is used as the anchor by which we determine if we are getting a good deal or not. We use comparable prices, "comps" to determine if the price of real estate is reasonable. At the gas pump the media not only introduced us to a $5.00 anchor, but they also gave us a *"super anchor"* of $7 to $10 to make us feel good about just spending $5.00. As we hear the $5.00 price repeatedly it soaks in, and we become comfortable with it.

Anchoring is a new term for most sales professionals. The prospective buyer comes to your office with an anchor in his or her mind that he or she will use to determine the reasonability of your pricing. If your price is a great deal higher than they're expecting to pay, they experience sticker shock, which has little or nothing to do with what they can or cannot afford. They're just shocked because their anchor was set at a lower price. Even though they like you and appreciate the services you've given them, they believe that you're overpriced, and will probably put off a decision to purchase. Let's face it, you wouldn't pay $2500 for a product you thought was worth $495, would you?

Let's analyze how the buyer established an anchor for the price of your product or services before he or she came into your office. If you needed a new refrigerator, and newspaper ads showed stores offering them in the $700 range, you would expect to pay around $700 when you went out to purchase one.

When people who need a product or service read the newspaper or watch TV infomercials and especially the internet, they don't miss the advertisements related to their needs. Almost all advertisements featuring price, offer low-priced products.

"Have you ever seen a product or service ad offering a product or service at the price you charge for yours?"

When the prospective buyer shows up at your office, they know that they have a need, and they are planning to buy. They come in expecting to spend their money for your product or service and they often think that price is excessive. The anchor in their mind is somewhere equal to the price ads they have seen. They come in expecting to spend a few hundred dollars to satisfy their need and your price is several thousand dollars. . . and they experience sticker shock. Not finding an anchor that makes sense they become confused and that's when the objection game begins. You start hearing meaningless objections which you try to overcome, but, in this state of confusion, they will not make a decision to purchase.

The good news is you can reset their Anchor.

If you go to a restaurant, open the menu, and see a steak at $65, after you gasp, you look further and find a steak for $50. If you wish to have a steak, you most likely will order that one. A basic rule of Anchoring is: The introduction of a higher price causes a lower price to seem reasonable, even if it isn't. Large restaurant chains employ a person called a "menu engineer," whose job it is to get us to spend more money. If, for example, they have a bottle of wine on the menu for $100 and it's not selling, they don't lower the price, they put a bottle on the menu for $200, which becomes the anchor, and immediately they start selling the $100 bottle. The $35 bottle now seems cheap, even when the consumer realizes that they can buy the same bottle of wine at the grocery store for $9.5o.

If you are to motivate a prospective buyer to purchase, you must remove their preconceived anchor and replace it with a new, more realistic one. If you wish to use this dynamic close, you must first create a price booklet.

Start with the cover.

<u>Your Company Name</u>

CONFIDENTIAL PRICE BOOKLET

EFFECTIVE DATE

On Page 1: List all the products you wish to sell. Show the prices for different levels of products or services.

<u>Economy Class</u> . . . $ printed in black (lowest price)

<u>Good Class</u> . . . . $ printed in blue (higher price)

<u>Best Class</u> . . . . $ printed in green (higher than blue)

<u>Specialty Class</u> . . . . $ printed in red (very high price)

(The price difference between of the product in green and the product in blue should be the amount of your discount)

Page 2: Explain some details related to the color of your choices.

Go into detail to establish that products or services on the price page in **Green** and **Blue** are our most popular products and services and the green products are much better than those in blue.

Now that you have a price booklet, let's go back to your presentation with the prospective buyer, only this time we'll add an extra step. Keep in mind that what we must do is to remove their unrealistic price anchor, replace it with a new realistic price anchor. We also introduce a "super-anchor."

This step must be introduced in the beginning of your presentation. You may say, *"Before we get started do you have any questions?* If they have questions, answer them. After you answer their questions or if they have no questions, you say, *"Over the years I have discovered that most people sitting in your situation have three questions in mind."*

"First, they want to know, **"Do I need the product?**

We will answer that question for you as we go. Second,

If I need the product, will the product I'm considering fill my needs? *We will also answer that question as we go. And third,* **If I have a need, and if this product or service will help, how much will it cost?"**

"Regarding the price, most salespeople wait until the end to tell you the cost. I like to give you an idea in the beginning." You then reach over for… **The Price Booklet**

Note: At this point, you haven't made your presentation , so you're not giving him or her a price trying to close the sale; you're just giving them information. They accept the information you offer without any pressure related to decision-making. Your conversation goes like this, *"This is our price booklet."* (The prospective buyer now feels they're going to get a peek behind the curtain.) *"You'll notice the effective date is November 2022. Because of the recession, we haven't raised our prices in over a year."*

Open to the first page, which is a menu of products and prices, and say,

"Notice this first economy class model, printed here in black, is $_____. Now I must be honest with you and tell you I haven't sold one of these economy products in years. The reason is they just don't solve the problem properly. This is the type of product you see advertised in the paper from time to time. Companies sometimes offer them for even lower prices. The truth is those companies seldom sell them; they just use them to get people to come into their office. We have them if someone wants one."

Note: We just removed the prospective buyer's preconceived anchor by letting him or her know that cheap products won't solve their problem, and the price they were considering is unrealistic. I call the economy product a shopper stopper. If a person is shopping and is planning to check out the inexpensive product they saw in the paper, you just removed their reason. Continue the conversation with, *"Now if you look down here at the bottom of the page, printed in red, you'll see our most expensive product which costs $_____. [new anchor] I seldom sell these expensive products. Only a few needs require all the bells and whistles. The products we sell most of the time are printed in blue, which are $_____, and our best product printed in green, which are $_____."*

You now turn the page…

The prospective buyer and the third-party are now experiencing sticker shock and may not hear what you say for a short while. They're probably thinking about the product printed in red! Wow, that's a lot higher than we expected. And those products I've seen in the paper for the economy price won't do the job. I wonder if I can get by with those printed in blue?" The salesperson will probably try to sell me the one printed in green. The more they think about the prices you just gave them, it soaks in and the more comfortable they become with those prices, just like you when you're at the gas pump. You're now on the next page.

You explain,

These products in blue and green are our most popular, so they now begin to see themselves paying the price of the products in blue or green. They would like to pay the lower price but, expect that you'll try to sell them the higher priced one.

Turn the page…At this point you must sell the benefits and justify the prices of those products printed in blue and green.

Leave the booklet sitting on the desk with the price page in view and continue with your usual presentation. You have now removed the preconceived anchor and replaced it with a new one. Talking about the price helps bring the price into prospective buyers' comfort zone. You have most of your presentation still ahead of you, but when you get to the end, the prospective buyer will be somewhat comfortable with the price, and you'll find it much easier for you to close the sale, especially if your sales price is lower than they now expect! With anchoring you can use,

The "Price booklet" Close

When it's time to close the sale, you may say,

"This is a very good time for you to have come in because during these three days we are conducting a special program." Let me explain what that means to you. *"The owner of this company is very smart and periodically he or she offers these programs, with the hope of building their patient base. The owner knows that if he or she adds new patients to his or her patient-base, and then takes great care of them, they will refer their family and friends to them. The owner has given me the authority, during these 3-days only, to give you a free upgrade. I can charge you the price of the products printed here in blue, and when we deliver, your product, he or she will deliver to you our very best product, which is printed here in green—so you're saving approximately* $_____. (the difference in price between the product printed in blue and the product printed in green.) *You get our very best product or service at our very best price and our owner gets a happy new patient. Does that make sense to you?"* It's important that the salesperson making this presentation explain the differences between the products listed in the

different colors and explain why the product in green is much better than the products in blue. It takes a little work to figure out the pricing, but it is worthwhile. Your explanation should be kept to a few one-liners. Mention the features briefly and accentuate the benefits.

Tell them what time it is, not how to build a clock!

Don't Become a TB!

A young man and his sweetheart went to the courthouse to get married. The judge told them they would have to go to the county clerk and get a license. A few weeks later, the couple returned to the courthouse with license in hand. The judge noticed a transposed letter in the bride-to-be's name, so he told them to go back to the clerk and have it corrected. A few months later, they returned, only to have the judge send them back to the clerk to have the date changed. A year passed before they returned to the courthouse. This time they were accompanied by a young child. They told the judge it was their child. The judge then explained, *"I can marry the two of you; however, the boy will technically be a bastard."* The young man replied, *"Interesting your honor, a technical bastard is exactly what the county clerk called you."* Remember:

People want to know how much you care...

Before they care how much you know.

And you won't show the prospective buyer how much you care by telling them how much you know.

A person who's good at closing the sale has a better than 80 percent closing rate; meaning over eighty percent of the potential buyers they see purchase their products or services! It's also important to understand that these presentations aren't complete presentations. These presentations focus on the close.

CHAPTER NINE

The "I Want to Think It Over" Objection

Have you ever gone into a store, with money in your pocket to buy a product, but the salesperson confused you to the point that you left without making the purchase? I went to a stereo store in the mall. All they sell is stereo equipment. I was in need and wanted to buy an expensive stereo. When approached by the salesperson, I told him what I had in mind. The salesperson took me on a tour of shelves and shelves of sophisticated equipment. He explained much more than I needed to know. He changed me from a consumer who knew what he wanted into a consumer who was confused and unsure of what he wanted. The choices were too many, so I told him "I want to think it over," and left.

I went to another store where the salesperson, after listening to what I wanted, took me over to one stereo and told me a few understandable reasons why this stereo was one of the best on the market to fill my need. I not only bought the stereo recommended, but also felt I got the best and was happy with my purchase.

"I want to think it over" can be a very difficult objection to overcome. You must convince the prospective buyer that it is in his or her best interest to do it now without giving him or her the feeling that he or she is being pressured. If you appear pushy, the prospective buyer will become irritated and leave. If you just sit there and don't attempt to close, the prospective buyer will not be irritated, but they will still leave. So how can we get past this objection and close the sale? When a person says, *"I want to think it over,"* we must determine the source of their uncertainty. The whole idea is to change the, "I want to think it over" objection, which is usually a stall hiding the true objection, to an objection you can handle, and then motivate the prospective buyer to purchase.

If you ask, *"What do you want to think over?"* the prospective buyer will generally answer with, *"Everything, or Nothing in particular; I just like to think things over before making a decision."* In either case, the objection is now set in concrete and is more difficult to overcome.

The solution is simple: Start by agreeing. *"It's always wise to think things over.* Then ask, *"how long have you been thinking about this?"* Then ask a two-part question with no pause so that the prospective buyer will focus on and answer the second half of the question, not the first. *"What is it you need to think over? Are you not convinced you have a need?"* If his answer is *"No,"* then you must go back and present more evidence to prove the need exists. If the prospective buyer says, *"Yes, I believe I have a need,"* you then ask, *"Are you concerned that the need can't be solved?"* If the answer to that question is *"yes,"* then you must demonstrate your product and or give the prospective buyer a greater sense of security by explaining your minimal-risk program. If the answer is in some negative form, you now ask: *"Are you concerned about the price?"* If the buyer says, *"Well, that's a lot of money,"* you need to explain: *"It is my job to find a solution that fulfills your need within your budget."* Offer other products at a lower price or explain how financing will make the price affordable. If he says, *"No, it's not the money!"* you may then ask, *"Are you just concerned about how your wife or husband feels about this?"* If the answer is *"yes,"* enlist spousal assistance. If the answer is, *"no,"* then try the,

The Three-Question Close

The Three-Question Close works well with the I want to think it over objection. You say, *"When my wife and I have an important decision to make, we always ask ourselves three questions. First, "Do we need the product?"* I believe you realize you need this solution, right? The second question is, *"Can I trust the company who makes the product?"* Well, in your case, that's the XYZ Company!" (Explain why you are selecting this company.) *"I can order your product from one of several manufacturers. The reason I have chosen the XYZ Company is their service. You and I are going to have a long relationship and if a problem comes up, I want to be sure that the company will* fix it. XYZ has the best service in the industry."

The third question is, *"Do I like and trust the salesperson who will be delivering this product and giving me service when I need it? You do have to place your trust in someone. I have been selling this product right here in (name your city) for x years, and I'm going to be here to take good care of you. Do you feel you can place your trust in me?"* The buyer should say, "Yes." Your response: *"Well then, let's get you started."* Ask a closing question! And,

> . . . ***Close the Sale!***

You may wish to use,

The Green-Lights Close

The Green-Lights Close works well when the buyer can't seem to make up his or her mind. The decision is too big, so the buyer must wait a while and think it over or talk it over with someone. He or she would do almost anything to keep from making the decision now.

You say, *"Sometimes a person will look down the street of life at all the lights turning red and green and say, 'When all the lights turn green, I'll go like heck all the way to the end.' But life doesn't work that way. With that approach, we would never get anywhere. What we must do is to start down the street, and the lights will change as we go."*

"The way to solve this problem is similar, we won't solve it if we do nothing. We need to take it one step at a time. First, we need to take some measurements. Then we need to pick some colors, then it will take about a week for your product to be built. At that time, I will call you and set up the delivery date. You have everything to gain and nothing to lose. Does that make sense to you?" With a yes answer,

. . . Close the Sale!

The Inducement Close

Or maybe you will use the Inducement Close.

After trying another motivation, if the prospective buyer says he or she must still think it over, try this approach:

"When a person says he or she wants to think over a problem that has existed for many months or maybe years, do you know how long they usually

think it over? Usually for about ten minutes. Do you know when they think it over? As soon as they leave the office! Then the problem is that if a question comes up, there is no one to ask for an answer. So why don't I leave the room and let the two of you discuss it?"

When you return, come prepared with a slightly different solution to get you back into conversation. If you return and ask, *"Did you make a decision?"* They may say, *"Yes and the answer is no."* If you return and say, *"I have come up with a slightly different solution. What we might do is…"* You are now back on closing grounds and this time they may not need to think it over.

CHAPTER TEN

The "Negative Previous Experience" Objection

A negative previous experience may have come in one of many forms. It is necessary to find out which form your prospective buyer has experienced, so you may deal with it.

Finding out what negative experience occurred usually happens because of being a good listener. The prospective buyer or the spouse may, early in the presentation, say something like: "I read a story in the paper about your product and why they cost so much. I saw something on TV about an operation that helps you, so you don't have to buy your product. I tried this product before, and it didn't work for me." My friend bought an expensive product and he or she doesn't like them."

These statements probably represent only half-hearted objections, or the prospective buyer wouldn't be sitting in front of you, considering your product or service. Nonetheless, these statements must be satisfied before the sale can be made. This objection is the prospective buyer's way of asking how your product or service has improved. They want you to assure them that they won't be disappointed, and that what happened to their friend won't happen to them. In the case of a friend's negative experience, explain how all needs are different. Ask, "What problem does your friend have?" They don't usually know, and the problem is lessened. The "Most Important Decision" close works well here.

CHAPTER ELEVEN

The "I have no need" Objection

A prospective buyer must need what you are selling. There may be times where there's nothing you can do to help the prospective buyer. However, if the prospective buyer's need is there, but they don't see the value in what you offer, you're the one at fault. Either you're not resonating, not exploring all possible needs, or not addressing the right need.

Obviously if the prospective buyer says, *"I'm not sure that my need is bad enough"* at the end of your presentation, you have not exposed the need sufficiently. You must now go back and ask a few more questions to better understand why this prospective buyer is sitting in front of you.

Here is a little story that may help the person who does not think or does not want to admit their need: *"First we must ask ourselves, is the problem getting better or is it getting worse? I have found that most problems* get worse with time, and we may be putting off the inevitable. While reading the newspaper, if a person begins to have difficulty seeing the print, they sometimes hold the paper farther away. When the paper reaches the end of their arms, then it's time to decide. They can do one of three things: they can decide not to read the paper anymore, which means they give up a lot of enjoyment. They can blame the newspaper company and tell them if they want me to take their paper, they will have to make the print larger, which they won't do. Or they can make the right decision, accept the problem as their own, and get glasses."

I often told this story to make the point: "When Roy Rogers turned 80, he decided to record an album. Upon hearing about it, many country singers wanted to sing along with Roy—Willie Nelson, Randy Travis, and Clint Black, to name a few. Each performer went to a studio and recorded their part of the recording and sent it to Roy. Roy then traveled to Nashville to record his part. Roy was seated in a small sound room, where he was to sing along with the music being piped in through earphones. Problem was that when he put the earphones on over his hearing aids, his hearing aids fed back. Roy then removed his hearing aids, put the earphones on, and then turned up the volume. Roy Rogers Jr. (Dusty) repeatedly entered the room to tell his dad that he was singing off-key. Frustrated, Roy decided to call the whole thing off and returned home. Dusty called me and explained the problem. I had a set of hearing aids without vents built for Roy. He returned to Nashville and finished the recording, and the album "Tribute" was soon released. We control how we speak by how we hear. When Roy could not hear properly, he sang off-key. Once we discovered the problem, we understood the need and corrected it.

Now I realize that story probably won't work for you but, maybe you have a story of your own that will create urgency to proceed. Once you gain approval of one prospective buyer, they will refer you to their friends.

CHAPTER TWELVE

The "I Want to Talk It Over" Objection

If the prospective buyer says, "I want to talk it over with a third-party," then you have already done something wrong. Place more emphasis on third-party attendance when the appointment is being made and ensure the third-party participates in your presentation.

If you find yourself in a situation where the third-party is absent, and you decide to continue with the presentation, you should ask a few questions before beginning. First ask, *"Is your third-party the reason you are here?"* If the answer is *"yes,"* then say, *"So your third-party wants you to solve your need? Do you think it will make your third-party happy if you solve this problem?"* You may ask if they wish to call the person they want to talk it over with while they are with you so you can answer any questions the person may have.

If you feel the prospective buyer makes his or her own decisions, you are well on the way to a successful close. Obviously, if one is comfortable making decisions on their own, such as a newly married senior who spends his or her own money, the closing is not an arduous task.

. . . Close the Sale!

CHAPTER THIRTEEN

The "I Want to Wait a While" Objection

The "I Want to Wait a While" objection is a cover-up for some other reason for not buying today. Maybe the prospective buyer does not feel he has enough of a need. Maybe he does not want to tell you he believes he needs that which you are selling but cannot afford it. By asking questions, you will bring out the true objection.

If the "I Want to Wait a While" objection is the only objection given, then you must convince the prospective buyer that waiting is not in his or her best interest. Use the Green-Lights Close.

CHAPTER FOURTEEN

The "I Want to Check My Insurance First" Objection

K now which insurance program will pay for what. Help the prospective buyer receive any benefit he or she has coming. It usually takes a phone call to the insurance company.

If you know the prospective buyer's insurance will not pay anything, say: "Let's look it up in our insurance schedule." After you look it up, you say: "With that insurance you save $xx." You must, of course, set up your company's Insurance Discount Schedule. Your price must include funds to cover an insurance discount and still make an acceptable profit. Then list every known type of insurance followed by a discount amount.

When the prospective buyer asks, "Will Medicare help?" You say: "Let's look it up in our Insurance Discount Schedule. Medicare doesn't pay anything; however, if you have your Medicare card, we can save you $xx." You then use the Sir Isaac Newton close or the,

The "Hillel" Close

(Hillel the Elder-110 BC–10 AD, was a Jewish religious leader who was born in Babylon and lived in Jerusalem during the time of King Herod; he is one of the most important figures in Judaic history.)

The Hillel Close will help with the person who just needs a little encouragement to make the decision. Obviously, it works best if your prospective buyer is Jewish or otherwise knows of Hillel. You say: *"Twenty-five-hundred years ago, the Jewish Rabbi Hillel said, 'If I am not for myself, then who will be for me? If I am only for myself, then what am I? If not now, when?' When we put off solving a problem, we are just putting off the inevitable."* Then explain, *"All we can work with today is the problem as it is. The sooner we get started, the better we can do. Your problem is not going away, it will probably worsen with time, and it is unwise to put off until tomorrow that which should be done today. For me to assist you, you must decide to help yourself. And the best time is now.* **Does that make sense to you?"**

Using the proper close at the right time takes practice. As you use them more often, they will become second nature, and your timing will improve. You will soon learn which close best answers which prospective buyer's objection. Your closing ratio will then improve.

CHAPTER FIFTEEN

The "I Want to Shop Around" Objection

The "I Want to Shop Around" objection is always a put-off. The prospective buyer is telling you he or she is not sold—or he or she may be sold and wants to negotiate the price. By asking leading questions, you may find out more about what your prospective buyer plans to go shopping for. Explain that you can get almost any product available and that you have products at many different prices, so he or she may shop without leaving your office. Explain that when a person goes shopping, all he or she will be comparing are the stories told and not the product of service they will receive.

Try the Most Important Decision close, if this doesn't work, before the prospective buyer leaves your office, *ask, "Is it price you are shopping for?" If the answer is "yes,"* then you may want to negotiate. Start by saying: *"Once I find out what you want to spend, I can tell you how* we can fulfill your needs. Before you came in today, what did you expect to spend?" or "I don't mind negotiating, as a matter of fact, I believe it is smart to negotiate. I negotiate on almost everything I buy. What price are you looking for?"

If a price is given and it is acceptable to you, you use the,

The "If I Could, Would You?" Close

The "If I Could, Would You?" close is simple and easy to use. If the prospective buyer makes you an offer, acceptable or not, you say: "If I could accept your offer, would you be ready to do it now?" If he says "No," you may just be wasting time and effort. If he says "yes," then proceed with the negotiation. If the offer is acceptable say: "Let's get started." If his offer is unacceptable say, "First let me say I appreciate negotiators—I am one myself. It makes sense to make the best deal you can. I cannot fill your needs properly for what you have offered, and I don't want to sell you something that won't fulfill your need but let me tell you what I can do."

You now make your counteroffer, ending with a closing question such as: "Does that sound fair to you?" Then take appropriate action and,

. . . **Close the Sale!**

If you don't come up with a Shopper Stopper, at a smaller percent of profit, your competitor will learn how you failed and make the sale. You will have gained nothing for your efforts.

Once again, REMEMBER:

Don't turn a statement, "WOW! These things are expensive," into an objection to be overcome.

Respond to a statement with a statement, *"Yes, everything is too expensive these days. I can remember when gas was 19 cents a gallon, but that's the way life is."* Then use the Physical-Action close. If you believe the money objection is just a smokescreen; you may want to use the Easy Question close.

CHAPTER SIXTEEN

Assume Buying Consent

Although closing the sale is the part of the job that nearly every salesperson dreads, it can be the easiest part of the process if you assume "buying consent" which starts with the forming of an attitude. You *must* believe that the prospective buyer has come to you for a solution to their need or want. Closing the sale is not asking a single question, giving one analogy or an individual act: it's the culmination of many questions, analogies and actions starting with the first hello. Don't fear the close. Do what you fear, and the fear will disappear. Remember: Because they try to close the sale more often, successful closers fail more than failures fail! When you're ready to close, the prospective buyer is usually ready to buy.

Closing Is a Process of Motivation

First, we must agree on this important premise: Motivating a person with a proven need for your product or service into accepting it is in that person's best interest. Developing a successful business and deriving a profit is but a positive byproduct of this process.

You may believe that you are a great salesperson, who gives great service, but you just can't close the sale! Guess what? If you are involved in a commercial business and you can't motivate the prospective buyer to purchase, then you have a serious problem. If you can't close the sale, then no one will benefit from your great skills.

Activity does not mean accomplishment. It is the nature of the sheep to be a follower wherever the leader goes. The Processionary Caterpillar is a follower even more so than the sheep. In 1896, the French naturalist, Jean Henri Fabre, conducted an experiment in which he collected a number of these caterpillars and placed them in a circle atop a large vase. These fuzzy little creatures lived up to their name in that they traveled single file, each touching with its head the rear of the one in front of it, around the rim of the vase. In this closed circuit, there was no longer a leader. Within a hand's-breadth lay a pine-branch, the tiny creature's meal of choice. The caterpillars walked for seven days and seven nights until their strength gave out entirely. Hungry and tired, they fell to the floor. The caterpillars to their misfortune, misinterpreted activity to mean accomplishment.

Salesmanship is a mix between product information and the gentle art of persuasion. How much is product information and how much is the gentle art of persuasion is an interesting consideration. Both are important. If you do not completely understand your product or service, the odds against success are overwhelming. If you only understand the product or service and fail to grasp the significant importance of the gentle art of persuasion, you will not motivate the prospective buyer to purchase. Like the Processionary Caterpillar, your activity will go unrewarded, and nothing will be accomplished. If you can't motivate the prospective buyer to purchase, you are a professional visitor, and no one will pay you for the sale that you almost made.

If you find it difficult to motivate the prospective buyer to purchase, I recommend that you learn a good close or two with which you are comfortable, and then practice. The more you have practiced the language, the more confident you will become and the easier it will be. If you have handled your presentation properly, you will often close the sale without hearing an objection. You handled them all in your presentation.

The reason for not purchasing now may vary from buyer to buyer. One closing strategy will not fit all. If the only tool you have in your tool chest is a hammer, then everything starts looking like a nail; the more closes you have mastered the greater your success.

It's true that you can lead a horse to water, but you can't make him drink. A good close simply adds a little salt to his oats!

The next few chapters are a number of tried and proven closes I recommend you commit to memory for use when the need arises.

CHAPTER SEVENTEEN

The "Ponce De Leon" Close

This is a close I often used to sell better hearing; you may find a way to say something similar in your profession.

Most people don't want to wear glasses or dentures or walk with a cane, and most don't want to wear hearing aids. Almost everyone would, however, like to turn the clock back and regain his or her youth.

I would say: *"Recently, I was chatting with a 95-year-old patient. She had a good sense of humor and, while laughing, said, 'As soon as I find Ponce De Leon's fountain of youth, I'm going to be young again."* I asked her, *"Don't you think that man has discovered the fountain of youth to some degree? For example, how old would you be if you didn't wear glasses? Could you drive a car? Could you read a menu?"* At first, I didn't think she understood what I meant, and then she said, *"Listen, I have one artificial knee and an artificial hip. I wear false teeth and glasses. If it were not for the things man has developed, I would be a half-blind, crippled old lady in a wheelchair sucking soup through a straw."* I would then explain, *"When you purchase hearing aids, you buy time. You probably won't hear as you did at age 10, but maybe we can turn your clock back eight to 10 years and, hopefully, you will hear as you did eight to 10 years ago. You would like that, wouldn't you?"* When the patient said, "Yes," I took appropriate action and, . . . **Closed the Sale!**

CHAPTER EIGHTEEN

The "Rush-Order" Close

The Rush-Order Close is usually tied to an important upcoming event, such as Mother's Day, a birthday party, Thanksgiving, or Christmas. If you are not careful, these upcoming events may become the reason to put-off buying until later. Before the prospective buyer brings up an upcoming event as an objection, you say: *"The good news is that if I send this order in today on a rush-order basis, we will have your product, or start your service in time for you to enjoy it during the holidays with your family. Won't that be great?"* The answer to this easy question will probably be yes. This closing technique gives prospective buyers a hard deadline to make their decision. You can reference policy changes or upcoming regulatory changes beyond your control that may prevent the prospective buyer from getting the current offer. For instance, you can offer additional discounts, features, or services. Time constraints make people decide faster. The rush order technique makes use of this aspect of human psychology. By giving a tight deadline, it increases the chances of closing a sale. You may say, *"I just found out that one of our other accounts had to push back their install a month. We have a spot in our schedule for the team to come to install your new product or service next week instead of in six weeks as I told you before.* **Should I put you on the schedule?"**

CHAPTER NINETEEN

The "Now or Never" Close

This is a traditional sales closing technique that invokes a "fear of missing out" to the prospective buyer. It creates a sense of urgency by adding "special, limited time offers." The goal is to give your prospective buyer that extra nudge needed to move to a yes.

For example, you can explain to them that only a few items are left in stock, and since it is a limited-edition product, they won't be able to buy it later. You can also use trigger words like "last chance", "ends soon", "today only", "don't delay", etc.

Example script:

"I should let you know that we have a special x% discount available for those who sign up this week. I wouldn't want you missing out on that."

In general, prospective buyers love having options. That's why they keep evaluating products to find the best of the best deals. But at the same time, they're also wired to avoid losing out on things. And that's why the now or never technique of closing sales works on the prospective buyers who need just one more reason to make that decision.

CHAPTER TWENTY

The "Puppy Dog" Close

The Puppy Dog close is a simple yet effective closing technique. The idea is to offer qualified prospective buyers a chance to try your product or service for themselves hands-on. Once they've spent some time experiencing its value, they won't want to hand it back. This experience gives them a chance to become attached and sure of their decision to adopt your solution. However, the closing technique can only apply in certain situations. You must determine if the prospective buyer can afford the product or service they will be trying. This is an effective method that uses a prospective buyer's love of the product to get them to buy it. It builds on the idea that few people who take a puppy home for a few days will give the puppy back. If you can "test drive" or "try before you buy," then you give the prospective buyer a chance to use your product and fall in love with it.

The Puppy Dog Close might start with something like this:

"If you would like to try our product or service for a month for free with no obligation to buy, I can ship one to you on Monday. If you don't like it, just ship it back to me. Would you want to give our product a try?"

A better approach is to have the prospective buyer pay for your product before the trial with your guarantee they will receive a full return of their money if they return the product. (You may have a small charge if they cancel.)

CHAPTER TWENTY-ONE

The "Options" Close

The Option Close is a traditional sales closing technique that has the prospective buyer choose between products you offer. It is best for situations where you feel easing the prospective buyer into the closing process would be beneficial to the relationship.

The option close offers 2 options from which to choose. It is a choice between something and something and both have "yes" answers.

Another example of what you might do: *"We could do the first installment at the end of this week or the beginning of next month. Which would be better for you?*

Another example that might sound like this:

"Well, now that you know what's available, which package would you like better, the starter package, the complete package, or the premium package?"

CHAPTER TWENTY-TWO

The "Take-Away" Close

T he Take-Away Close involves reviewing features of your offer and then suggesting that the prospect forgo some of the elements to save money (or time, or hassle, etc.).

It plays upon the fact that we, as humans, hate to lose something, whether we own it yet or not.

You may suggest that taking something away can make the prospective buyer want to move ahead with the sale, so they don't lose anything on their wish list.

The Take- Away Close might work like this:

"I know we discussed the wireless version of the product, but for how you intend to use the product, the wireless function might not be necessary. Also, the portable charger wouldn't be vital either since you will primarily use it in one place. What you lose in versatility saves you a few dollars every month. Does that make sense to you?"

CHAPTER TWENTY-THREE

The "Ben Franklin" Close

The reason this technique is called The Ben Franklin Close is because it involves a pros and cons list. Back in the day Ben Franklin used to love making pros and cons lists.

These lists are an effective tool for getting your thoughts on paper and figuring out what's important and what you're worried about. The Ben Franklin Close works great for figuring out what your prospective buyer values, helps them think of all the positives, and helps them realize that the cons are a small price to pay for all the benefits.

Here is how It Works. This closing technique will only work if it's presented correctly. It's important to realize that the pros should outweigh the cons by at least 2 or 3 times. I recommend sitting down and writing out all the pros that your product or service provides to your prospective buyer. Feel free to get creative too! Sometimes your pros must be something you can't really measure, like how it makes your prospective buyer feel, the pain it'll diminish for them, etc.

Present the idea of making a pros and cons list when your prospective buyer isn't going with your offer. The objection might be the price, sleeping on it, thinking about it, etc. Basically, you use this close when you get a difficult objection that requires logic and breaking down the offer.

You may say, *"I understand you want to go home and think about this. I completely agree with a decision as important as this; however, it won't change the fact that you'll have to at least make sure that the pros outweigh the cons. Now, before you go can we work on one together?"*

You'll want to use this close when your prospective buyer is right in front of you because you can pull out their objections and start to overcome them. It's always best to work towards the solution together and it'll help your prospective buyers trust you more. Try to get the prospective buyer to come up with the pros and cons themselves. You might have to get the ball rolling but once you do let them do all the talking. It's important because you might state something that's a pro for you but a con for them. You might think your 2-week delivery time frame is awesome but unaware that your competitor has 3-day delivery. You might think your price is very low and fair, but it is most likely the thing holding up the sale.

Once you make a list to get all the pros and cons out you can start to add value. I recommend finding out what the current list is worth to your prospective buyer in terms of dollars. That way you can work on bridging the gap between what your prospective buyer believes it's worth and what the actual cost is. This is important because if your product or service costs $10,000 but the prospective buyer is stuck at $9,500, you aren't selling $10,000, you're selling $500. The gap is a lot more manageable from a sales perspective.

You can add value by thinking up some more pros. Remember that some pros might be worthless to your prospective buyer. For this reason, you should ask something like "what's that worth to you?" after adding another pro. Keep going until you run out of pros.

Once you get the value to outweigh the cost is when you get the sale. Just make sure you ask for it! The best way to ask for the sale during this close is to ask for the close looking for a **no** answer. It'll help you close the sale because the word "no" puts your prospective buyer at ease and gives them the control. You can ask for the sale by saying something like, *"Now that we completed this list, are there any other reasons not to go ahead right now?"*

No means the sale is closed. Yes, means you'll have to ask what's holding it up and work to overcome that.

If you handle the Ben Franklin close correctly, you are bound to increase your closing rate.

CHAPTER TWENTY-FOUR

The "Summary" Close

With this technique, all you do is summarize the benefits the person will receive after they buy your service. You must be specific and tell them what their money is buying them. It must sound impressive and attractive. And then ask a closing question.

CHAPTER TWENTY-FIVE

Illustrative Analogy Closes

It's not always **what** *you say,*

it's how you say it!

S ome of these analogies make a good point...and a few just make good conversation. You could say, *"As I look into your eyes, time stands still!"* or *"You have a face that could stop a clock!"* Same thing, different words, entirely different meanings.

"Choose your words carefully."

Presenting an interesting analogy is a great technique for providing important information in an easy-to-understand format. The prospective buyer accepts information more comfortably when listening as you tell them how others have successfully solved their problems. Make sure that a third-party analogy makes your point, and, as often as you can, don't make a point without giving an interesting analogy. Depending upon where you are in your presentation, these analogies usually precede your attempt to close the sale. The words in each of these analogies have been carefully selected to make the correct point. They have been used and proven effective for many, many years. I recommend that you read them over and over and say them aloud until you have them memorized verbatim. Once you have committed the stories to your memory, I'm sure you'll find a place to use them. They have worked for me, and I'm sure they will work for you.

The " Sound-Sorter" analogy

This analogy worked well for the product I was selling but it shows how to use logic and emotion to close the sale.

The Sound-Sorter analogy may be used to close the sale at the end of most presentations. It may also be used to overcome most objections by placing importance on something other than the objection at hand. I consider the Sound Sorter analogy to be one of my best.

Roy Rogers did not like the idea of wearing eyeglasses or hearing aids. Pointing to a row of leather boots, which had a brightly embroidered thunderbird on each, he said, *"Look at those boots. Look how I am dressed. I look like what I am supposed to look like, the King of the Cowboys. Even though I may need them, I don't see the King of the Cowboys wearing hearing aids."*

I went through the Sound-Sorter analogy. As soon as I had finished, Roy took his hearing aids out of his pocket, put them in his ears and said, *"Guess I had better start getting used to them."*

You say: *"Seventy-eight (the prospective patient's age) years ago, when you came into the world, your most important possession was your brain, but it was empty. You had five senses: touch, taste, smell, vision and hearing. The purpose of your senses was to gather information and send it to your brain to be sorted and stored as knowledge. Everything you have stored in your brain today got there through your five senses. How sharp and alert you will be tomorrow will be determined, in part, by what your brain receives today.*

As I look at you, I see you as part of a picture. I can see in front of me and out to both sides. I can see in color, and I can even tell the texture of your clothing just by looking at it. While I'm looking at you, if I take hold of the edge of the table, my sense of touch tells me it's about one-inch thick and that it has a hard, smooth surface. If I take a taste of coffee, I can tell whether it's hot or cold, bitter, or sweet, and, in fact, if it is even coffee! If I smell something, I can tell where it's coming from. I can tell whether the smell is pleasant or foul, and I might even recognize what it is.

"Without turning my head, if someone speaks, I can tell you from which direction it is coming, whether it's a man or woman, old or young, happy, or sad, and whether the person is getting closer or going away. I may be able to recognize who is speaking by the sound quality of their voice. What is most amazing is that I can recognize these sounds as words by which we can communicate. It is man's ability to communicate that sets him apart from all other creatures on earth and gives him the power to rule the universe. You are 78. If you're like me, you have had many good times and a few you would like to go back and rearrange. But, of course, those 78 years are spent and cannot be changed. The challenge now is to make the rest of your life the best of your life. What you are deciding is whether you are going to accept hearing and feeding your brain only part of what is being said, or are you going to do what

I would do if I had your problem? I would have the best hearing instruments available. What would you like to do? Would you like to hear better?"

When the prospective buyer says, "yes," you say, *"Sit over here and let's get you started."*

The "Penny a Day" Analogy

This story explains how the prospective buyer may have developed a need without being noticed.

"There was once an elderly man who had a jar of pennies on his living-room table. Every day, his grandson took a penny. The loss of pennies went unnoticed until the jar was a third empty. Upon discovery, the elderly man proclaimed, 'Someone took a handful of my pennies last night.' Of course, he didn't lose a third of his pennies last night, even though it seemed that way. He lost them slowly but didn't notice. Well, that is how your need has developed—a little at a time over many years—and you probably didn't even notice it until a third of your need has developed. Does that make sense to you?"

The "Cooking a Bullfrog " Analogy

This next analogy may sound a little corny, but it has proven very effective when used at the right time. I often use it when the buyer, for whatever reason, believes that his or her need is not too bad or is denying that they have a need at all.

You say: *"You have what I call a problem cooking a bullfrog. Do you know how to cook a bullfrog? If you tried to put a bullfrog into a pot of boiling water, it would jump halfway across the room. What you must do is put the bullfrog in cold water where it's comfortable, and then turn up the heat. The bullfrog will slowly cook without even knowing it. If I could give you your problem in an instant, you would jump halfway across the room. Like cooking the bullfrog, your problem has come about so slowly that your loss developed without you even noticing it. Does that make sense to you?"*

. . . *Close the Sale!*

The "Foundation of Your Happiness" Analogy

The following close can help overcome the money objection.

You explain, "One time, a grandparent told me that the three things that are the foundation of your happiness, which you should always protect, are: Your health, the food on your table and the roof over your head. I have always believed that your health is the most important key to your happiness. Unfortunately, problems don't usually get better; they usually get worse with time. If purchasing this product won't take the food off your table or the roof from over your head, doesn't it make good sense that we get started in the right direction?"

. . . *Close the Sale!*

The "All-Your-Money-Back" Analogy

I have used the following method for years, and I can tell you that it works—and it will lower your cancelation rate!

You say, *"When you come in at the time of delivery, if I don't deliver all that I have promised, we will give you back every penny you have paid, and it will cost you nothing. If you don't receive what I have promised at the time of delivery, the mistake is ours, not yours, so you get all your money back. If you receive all that I have promised at the time of delivery it will get better as you get used to them. Does that make sense to you?"*

... Close the Sale!

The "I Hope You Like Me" Analogy

The following statement gives the prospective buyer and the third-party reassurance that you intend to take good care of the prospective buyer once he or she becomes *your* patient, client, or customer.

You explain, *"I hope you like me, because once you become my patient, client, or customer, I will be in your life for the rest of your life. Your need for service will not go away, and I've been here in (city) for (x) years, and I'll be here for you!*

... Close the Sale!

The "Spending Money on Yourself" Analogy

This next analogy helps with the money objection.

When talking about money, you say, *"When you spend money on yourself, you're not really spending it—you're changing it into something you'll enjoy more than the money. We spend our life saving for the rainy day. Well, it's raining! So why don't we get you started."*

... Close the Sale!

I realize that these analogies are not all in the context of presentations, some are random thoughts. I also realize that you as a skilled professional will find a use for some of these stories or thoughts as the need arises.

CHAPTER TWENTY-SIX

Mistakes to Avoid While Closing a Sale

Here are some of the basic principles that you should know before you apply any of these sales closing techniques. Think of them as principles on what salespeople should **never** do.

1. **Do not have poor communication etiquette**.

It includes chewing gum on calls, having background noise, or not speaking clearly. These can severely hurt the chances of closing a sale.

2. **Do not jump to conclusions**.

If a prospective buyer is unsure, it means that they have not decided yet. It does not translate to a yes or no. You can use the sales closing technique to move them to a yes, but do not assume.

3. Do not say you know something if you don't.

If you are unsure about the aspect of the product or service you are selling, you can always check and let them know. Prospective buyers appreciate honesty.

4. Do not be defensive.

This behavior is seen when it comes to pricing. Defending any aspect of the product or service may be a red flag for the prospective buyer. A better approach is to highlight the values they get from your offering. You can also give logical reasons on why different prospective buyers choose different options.

5. Do not be negative.

There will be rejections and objections while closing sales. That is why people have come up with different closing techniques. Be persistent and leave the door open for prospective buyers to return.

Wrap up!

To repeat myself, the closing techniques in this book are not just black and white that one will work, and another will not. There are no set rules related to the sales closing techniques. You can mix and match all these techniques and find out the best combo that works for you. The best-selling close for you might not work for your colleague, so make sure you sort out, through trial and error, the best ones that work for you and, don't fail. . . **Close the Sale!**

CHAPTER TWENTY-SEVEN

Avoiding Cancelations

Ask most people if they have trouble deciding, and they'll answer, "Well, yes and no." If they do decide yes, then they'll think they should have decided no, and vice versa. This is especially true for seniors who may feel insecure. Often, the one who made decisions in the long-time marriage is deceased. The living spouse may fear making a bad decision and will constantly change his or her mind. Whenever a new prospective buyer exhibits signs of decision remorse at the time of purchase, it's wise to counsel him or her about worrying.

I say it this way: *"Now, I want you to go home and forget all about this until we call you to come for delivery. So, don't worry, okay? If a friend or family member disagrees with your decision, then just have them with you at the time of delivery. I will be happy to explain your purchase and demonstrate all the details of your purchase with them."*

CHAPTER TWENTY-EIGHT

Seven Traits of a Successful Salesperson

There was once a salesperson named Simon Smith who was going to take the two o'clock boat to the isle of success. He went down to the seaport and purchased his ticket for the two o'clock departure. While waiting to board he decided to weigh himself on a nearby scale. He stepped onto the scale, put in his money, and down dropped his fortune.

It read, *"Your name is Simon Smith, you are five-feet-seven-inches tall. You weigh one hundred sixty-five pounds, and you are going to take the two o'clock boat to the isle of success."*

In disbelief he stepped off the scale and looked around for a camera but didn't find one. He then put on a hat and sunglasses and pulled his collar up and stepped back onto the scale. He put in his money, and down dropped his fortune.

It read, *"Your name is still Simon Smith, you still are five-feet-seven-inches tall. You still weigh one hundred sixty-five pounds, and you are still going to take the two o'clock boat to the isle of success."*

Wow! Now with greater disbelief, he then went into the restroom, opened his suitcase, and completely changed his clothes, came out and once again stepped onto the scale. He put in his money, and down dropped his fortune.

It read, *"Your name is still Simon Smith, you are still five-feet-seven-inches tall. You still weigh one hundred sixty-five pounds, but while wasting your time foolishly, you just missed the boat to the isle of success."*

Don't foolishly waste your time and miss the boat to greater success as a salesperson. The time for greater success as a salesperson is now! Here are the seven traits that I have found that successful practitioners have in common.

1- Sold on your Products and Services!

You must believe that the product or service you are selling is the best available to the prospective buyer!

2- Unlock the Power of Your Positive Mind!

Harry Houdini was considered one of the world's greatest escape artists. He was once summoned to the British Isles, where they had just finished constructing what they believed was the world's best jail. They believed that no one would ever escape. Houdini was paraded through town and put in jail, where he would try to escape. As soon as the town's leaders left, Houdini went to work. From the waistband of his trousers, he removed a long, thin metal wire and began picking the lock. After an hour had passed, Houdini, wet with sweat, became depressed and began to think that maybe this lock couldn't be opened. In his moment of frustration, he leaned against the door and the door fell open. Houdini couldn't unlock the lock because they had forgotten to lock it.

In life, many people perceive the doors of a positive, productive lifestyle as being locked for them. Successful people know that they can control their attitude and realize the doors were never locked in the first place. They understand that while they cannot control everything negative that happens, they *can* control their responses. No one needs a negative-thinking person to get them down: We can get down all by ourselves! We need others to raise us up. No matter how positive you may be; you can get better.

3- Continuous Effort!

A preacher driving along a country road stopped to view a beautiful farm sight: The fields were green with healthy vegetation. The rows were straight and long, the fences surrounding the farm freshly painted, and the farming equipment appeared well cared for and rust-free. Everything as far as he could see was picture-perfect. As the farmer on his tractor came near the fence, the preacher waved and shouted, "The Lord has surely been good to you!" The farmer shouted back, "Yes, you're right; the Lord has been good to me, but you should have seen this place when he had it all to himself!"

What would you rather have, a gift of a million dollars or a chance to work as a salesperson? Don't answer that! A million dollars is a lot of money!

There was once a man named Josh, who was about to inherit a million dollars. His lawyer thought that this exciting news might cause Josh, who had a history of heart problems, to die from a heart attack, so he asked Josh's minister to use psychology and give Josh the exciting news slowly. The preacher went to visit Josh and asked, "Josh, what would you do if you inherited a million dollars?" Without hesitation Josh replied, "Why, I'd give half of it to the church"...and the minister died from a heart attack! So, it only takes half a million dollars to kill a minister.

Being successful in the sales profession is not easy. It's very competitive, and there's no substitution for hard work. It takes effort to give a good presentation, and often a little extra effort can make the difference between doing good and doing great. The difference between closing or missing the sale. In baseball two feet is often the difference between a home run and an out! Along with hard work, you must work smart, making a continuous effort.

4- <u>C</u>onfidence!

Which comes first, success or confidence? I'm not sure, but I have found that one brings on the other. I have observed that the more competent a salesperson is, the more successful he or she will become and the more successful a person becomes, the more confident he or she will be.

There was once a salesperson who sold bulletproof vests—or at least that was the plan! His sales were very slow, and one day the sales manager called him into his office. He told the salesperson that his problem was that he wasn't confident about what he was selling. The salesperson disagreed, so the manager asked him to put on his demo bulletproof vest, which he did. Holding a loaded revolver aimed at the salesperson, the sales manager asked, *"Are you ready for this?"* Nervously the salesperson replied, *"Well, okay,"* and the sales manager shot him. The salesperson said, *"WOW, I didn't even feel that."* The salesperson went back out and became a great bulletproof vest salesperson.

Now I'm not sure that this story is true, but you get the point. This little demo gave the salesperson the next important trait of successful people.

5- Enthusiasm!

The last four letters in the word enthusiasm are "i-a-s-m" which I believe stands for "I am sold myself." Enthusiasm doesn't necessarily mean jumping up and down and being loud. Enthusiasm is an outward expression of your inner belief. If you don't get enthusiastically involved with solving the prospective buyer's need or want, the odds of success are slim. When you become enthusiastic about helping the prospective buyer, closing the sale becomes easy!

6- Set Your Course!

If you don't know where you are going, you'll probably get there. Think about yourself as a boat out in the ocean. If what you plan for is "a calm, no problem existence," no matter which way the wind blows, it will rock your boat. If you know where you want to go, occasionally you will find yourself in the middle of a favorable wind that will move you, towards that which you desire at an unbelievable speed. When you know where you're going, the journey will be much more successful.

A farmer once placed a small, growing pumpkin into a jar. As the pumpkin grew, it became the exact size and shape of the jar. People often poke themselves into small jars beyond which they cannot grow. They proclaim, *"One of these days I'll become great at closing the sale, as soon as..."* and then they pile up so many obstacles in front of themselves that, *"one of these days"* becomes *"none of these days."* If you have learned a few better ways to motivate the prospective buyer, use them in your next presentation.

And, even if you're a great actor, insincerity glows in the dark, and this leads us to the last key.

7- <u>S</u>incerity!

People want to know how much you care before they care how much you know. You cannot act sincere; you must be sincere. If you spend your days helping those get what they need and want, you'll acquire that which you need and want.

The first letter of these seven traits creates the acrostic "Success!"

<u>S</u>old on your Products and Services!

<u>U</u>nlock the power of your positive mind!

<u>C</u>ontinuous Effort!

<u>C</u>onfidence!

<u>E</u>nthusiasm!

<u>S</u>et your course!

<u>S</u>incerity!

Success comes in "cans," not in "cannots!"

Give love as a part of all you do…

Love

God gives to thee an abundance of love

Through friends and family, from heaven above.

Try as you will, all of your love to give

You'll have plenty still, for as long as you live.

For love is to share, and not meant to store;

Show others you care, and you'll always have more.

God did not place love in your heart to stay;

For love is not love, until you give it away.

- Roy Bain

From this moment on when someone asks you,

"How are you?"

Don't answer, *"I'm okay!"* Don't answer, *"I'm good."* Answer, **"I'm Fantastic!"** And when you get home after a day at work, hold up a glass of your favorite drink, and water is great, and say, **"I am Fantastic,"** and propose a toast to yourself! You might say,

"I am a great salesperson because I'm great at overcoming objections and closing the sale!"

Develop your Gentle Art of Persuasion!

don't fail . . .Close the Sale

And . . .

Make the rest of your life the best of your life!

Thank You!

772d7a19-0415-4b26-9da1-5675d4e4ff80R01